Maimonides. Essays and Texts
850th Anniversary

by
Norman Roth

Madison, 1985

ISBN 0-942260-59-7

To My Students, Past, Present and Future

Table of Contents

Abbreviations

b. (ben, ibn) = son of
B.B. = Baba Batra (Talmud)
B.M. = Baba Meṣi^{c}a (Talmud)
B.Q. = Baba Qamma (Talmud)
C.E. = Common Era
J.Q.R. = Jewish Quarterly Review
Jer. = Jerusalem Talmud
M.G.W.J. = Monattschrift für Geschichte und Wissenschaft des Judenthums
Meta. = Aristotle, Metaphysics
N.E., Nic. Ethics = Aristotle, Nicomachean Ethics
n.s. = new series
P.A.A.J.R. = American Academy for Jewish Research. Proceedings
R.E.J. = Révue des études juives
T. = Talmud

Introduction

Moses b. Maimon (1135-1204) was without doubt the greatest Jewish scholar of all time, who earned the well-deserved proverbial phrase: "From Moses (the lawgiver) to Moses, none arose like Moses."

He was never a rabbi, and earned his living as a physician; yet he became the greatest authority on Jewish law in the Middle Ages, and later codifications were based to a large degree on his work. His commentary on the Mishnah is still the most important ever done. His great code of Jewish law, the **Mishneh Torah**, was the only work he wrote in Hebrew and it remains a model of beautiful and simple Hebrew style. His Book of Commandments was accepted, with a few disagreements, as the authoritative classification of the 613 commandments of the Torah. His numerous medical works, including a multi-lingual dictionary of drugs, gained for him the reputation of the greatest medical authority of his time. What may be called his "theological" treatises (including a treatise on the Almohad persecution of the Jews and the proper response to it, the "Letter to Yemen" discussing the messiah, Christianity and Islam, and other such works) were widely read in his day and long afterward. His various writings on astronomy reveal a profound knowledge of this difficult subject, and are still studied by specialists. His philosophical *magnum opus*, the **Guide of the Perplexed**, earned for him the chief place among the many great medieval Jewish philosphers, and its influence not only upon Jewish thought but also upon the medieval Christian Scholastics is well known.

It is certainly most fitting that the world has decided to honor Maimonides, as he is known, in this 850th year of his birth. Celebrations and conferences are being held everywhere: Israel, Cairo, the United States, and especially in Spain—the land of his birth, where he received his education, and the land which he always considered his, even though he and his family were forced to flee the Almohad tyranny there.

During the course of this anniversary year, I was invited to present papers at various conferences in honor of Maimonides. The first of these, and the first conference to be held in this country to commemorate the anniversary, was a symposium at the University of Southern California in Los Angeles, under the direction of Prof. Moshé Lazar (March 27-28, 1985).

It seemed to me that this anniversary year should not be allowed to pass without one single volume being published in honor of Maimonides. The tasks involved in issuing the papers of conferences are well known to those who have worked on such things; requiring the revision of papers and adding of footnotes, editing, and the difficulties of finding a publisher and seeing the work finally through press. The result is usually a delay of years, by which time whatever excitement was generated by the event and its subject has long since passed. Hence, my decision to collect the various papers which are included in this volume, and to add to them some new material, including translations of some of Maimonides' own writings which appear here for the first time. The work necessarily had to be done in haste, and no doubt there are both omissions and errors as a result. The purpose is not the honor of the author, but the honor due to Maimonides.

The publication of this volume would not have been feasible were it not for the generosity, gracious support and hard work of the press of the Hispanic Seminary of Medieval Studies, Ltd. To all who worked on the manuscript, especially Prof. Lloyd Kasten, Prof. John Nitti, and Miss Ruth Richards, my deep gratitude. Also, of course, to Miss Barbara Granick, a graduate student in the Department of Hebrew and Semitic Studies, my thanks for her patience and endless effort in processing the manuscript for publication.

While making acknowledgements, I must certainly mention my continuous gratitude to the many scholars who have guided me and whose gracious support and friendship sustain and inspire me. Prof. Benzion Netanyahu, who first introducted me to the field of Jewish history and guided me through my graduate work, heads the list. The distinguished scholars of the Medieval

Academy of America, and its administrative staff, serve as a model of what gentlemen and scholars should be. I treasure my relationship with them and strive to be worthy of their confidence. A smaller group of colleagues who comprise the American Academy of Research Historians on Medieval Spain also are outstanding models, and it is both a pleasure and honor to be associated with them.

My thanks, too, to the Wisconsin Society for Jewish Learning, a unique and wonderful organization, and to the University of Wisconsin for their constant and generous grant support which has enabled this and other work to be completed.

It is a pleasure to acknowledge, too, the support of my colleagues Profs. Michael Fox, Keith Schoville, Gilead Morahg, Yair Mazor, and Emeritus Prof. Menahem Mansoor. Finally, my students, past, present and future, to whom this book is fondly and gratefully dedicated. May they and others benefit from it, and cherish the memory of Moses our teacher.

Norman Roth
University of Wisconsin

Introducing Maimonides to the English Reader

Moses b. Maimon, called Maimonides, whose 850th anniversary of birth is celebrated this year throughout the world, was undoubtedly the most important Jewish scholar of all time. Yet, aside from casual references to his **Guide** in a few (by no means all) books on medieval philosophy, and some few more careful studies of his influence on Thomas Aquinas and other medieval Scholastics, there is very little awareness of his work and his importance in non-Jewish circles. The result is not only that while students of medieval history become familiar at least with the names of Albertus Magnus, Duns Scotus, Thomas Aquinas and others, they almost never have heard of Maimonides. The general lack of awareness among even the educated public is appalling. An example of this in connection with one of the papers presented in this present collection is that the local Madison newspapers decided not to publicize the lecture because they made a decision that no one had ever heard of Maimonides! (Nevertheless, the lecture was well attended by at least some members of the University community.) Two sessions dedicated to the anniversary of Maimonides at the International Medieval Congress held at Kalamazoo in May of this year, with papers by highly respected scholars in the field, were almost completely ignored, so that we sat around talking to each other. One recalls the hundreds of people who attended sessions recently at that same Congress on the anniversary of St. Benedict, and it goes without saying that a St. Thomas anniversary would have enormous participation.

Yet there are Maimonides hospitals in numerous cities around the country, as well as various Jewish day schools named in his honor. In Milwaukee, the unique Wisconsin Society for Jewish Learning (a major benefactor of Jewish studies at the universities in Madison and Milwaukee) presents an annual Maimonides Award to an outstanding physician whose work exemplifies not only high ethical and professional standards, but who has made also a contribution to the understanding of Jewish culture.

For Jewish students and scholars, the importance of Maimonides is obvious (although it is no less sadly true that he is neglected as well by many of these), but why should those whose chief area of interest is not Jewish culture be concerned with him?

Maimonides, born and raised in Córdoba in Muslim Spain, was a product of that unique cultural environment. It was not unusual for Jews of medieval Spain to excel in more than one area of learning. Samuel Ibn Naghrillah, prime minister and commander-in-chief of Muslim Granada, was both a great Hebrew poet and authority in Jewish law; Solomon Ibn Gabirol wrote poetry and works of philosophy (as "Avicebrol" he was famous to medieval Christian Scholastics who wrongly thought him to have been a Christian, and read his "Source of Life" in Latin translation); Abraham Ibn Ezra wrote commentaries on the entire Bible, works on science and astronomy, philosophy, etc.

Yet Maimonides outshone them all in his brilliance and his accomplishments in a variety of fields. He composed a commentary on the entire *Mishnah*, parts of the *Talmud*, a treatise on logic, works on astronomy, a monumental fourteen-volume code of Jewish law (the **Mishneh Torah**), numerous responsa on legal and religious matters, various ethical and religious treatises, a dictionary of drugs in several languages, several volumes of medical works, and his famous philosophical work, **Guide of the Perplexed**. He even managed to write a few Hebrew poems, though he generally was opposed to poetry.

It would be difficult, if not impossible, to name another single scholar in history whose prolific output came close to equalling that of Maimonides. Indeed, his well-deserved reputation earned for him the proverb which was current in his own lifetime: "From Moses (the Lawgiver) to Moses (Maimonides), none arose like Moses."

Having established the prolific nature of his work, the question still remains to be answered, why should the non-Jewish specialist care about it. The answer lies, aside from the intrinsic merit of studying the product of any great genius, in the *necessity* (and not merely "desirability") of learning something about the Jewish civilization. The argument can be made—to my knowledge, it has not previously been made—that virtually all one could desire to know at least about pre-modern Jewish civilization can be found in these writings of Maimonides. The single element which apparently is lacking, biblical commentary, is only an apparent oversight; for in truth profound (and, admittedly, less profound) insights into the meaning of various biblical texts are scattered throughout his works.[1] Very important also is his contribution to the development and the style of the Hebrew language, with which one of these papers deals.

His philosohical and religious ideas are to be found not only in the **Guide**, but scattered also throughout his commentary on the *Mishnah* (especially in the various "Introductions" which he composed and which stand as almost independent treatises), his letters, and even in his medical writings. Together, these give a good insight into the nature of classical and medieval Jewish thought. He has much to say of interest for historical interpretation and even for comparative religion, in which he was one of the pioneers.[2] But it is especially his code of Jewish law which is of significance for an understanding of the entire scope of Jewish life and law, which embraces not only what moderns think of as "religion," but such areas as mental health, civil law, astronomy, and philosophical knowledge.

Maimonides wrote almost all of his work in Judeo-Arabic (i.e., Arabic written in Hebrew script), because this was the language most widely used and understood by the Jews of the Muslim world. The single exception was his code, **Mishneh Torah**, which he wrote in clear and simple Hebrew so that all Jews everywhere could use it. Neither of these languages, Arabic or Hebrew, is widely read and understood today, even among scholars. Fortunately, therefore, many of his works have been translated. Already in the medieval period, almost all of his Judeo-Arabic work was translated into Hebrew, some also into

Latin, and the **Guide** into Spanish and Italian. Over the course of centuries, other Latin translations were made of some work, editions with German translations of most of the commentary on the *Mishnah* (though these are of uneven quality; some excellent and some much less so), translations of the **Guide** into many languages, etc.

The purpose of the present brief essay is to present a survey of the available English translations, to enable the student familiar only with that language to know what is available. Even for scholars able to read other languages this guide may be useful, as the more modern English translations tend to be more readily available in libraries than are translations in other languages.

Code of Jewish Law (*Mishneh Torah*):

The entire work is slowly being translated and is in the process of publication by Yale University Press in its Yale Judaica Series. Several volumes have appeared so far. An introductory volume, not without serious problems, has recently appeared: Isadore Twersky, **Introduction to the Code of Maimonides** (1980). While this book unfortunately does not live up to its stated purpose, the first chapter (''Introduction'') is perhaps the most useful (see in general my critique of this book, reprinted in this present collection).

In addition to the Yale translation, individual volumes in other translations have appeared:

Book of Knowledge and **Book of Adoration**, tr. Moses Hyamson (1937; rpt. 1962), not entirely accurate.

The Book of Knowledge, tr. H. M. Russell and J. Weinberg (1981), better than the Hyamson translation but still not entirely correct.

An anthology of selections is **Maimonides' Mishneh Torah**, ed. Philipp Birnbaum (1967). Selections of some important sections, but unfortunately not newly translated, appear also in Twersky, **A Maimonides Reader** (1972).

Book of Commandments (*Sefer Ha-Miṣvot*):

This is Maimonides' classification of the 613 commandments of the Torah, with brief explanations. Often there is philosophical and religious material of great importance. The work has been translated as **The Commandments**, two volumes, by Charles Chavel (1967), a generally reliable translation.

Commentary on the Mishnah:

It is nothing short of outrageous that there exists no translation, in any language (other than Hebrew, of course), of this extremely important major work of Maimonides. As already noted, several doctoral dissertations in the latter part of the last century and the early part of this were done as editions (Judeo-Arabic) and translations (German) of individual tractates of the commentary. These are not only difficult to obtain, but of uneven quality.

In English, there is **Introduction to Seder Zeraim and Commentary on Tractate Berachoth**, tr. Fred Rosner (1975). This Introduction (often called generally "Introduction to the Mishnah") is one of the most important of Maimonides' treatises. Dr. (M.D., not Ph.D.) Rosner's translation is generally good, though based on the medieval Hebrew version and not the original Arabic text. It has the merit of notes which are informative without being pedantic, and it has a subject index.

An earlier English translation, not without merit, appeared in **Gal-Ed: Hebrew Review and Magazine of Rabbinical Literature** 1 (1834): 116-19, 129-35, 152-54, 163-66, 188-92, 232-35, 267-70.

The **Commentary to Mishnah Aboth**, tr. Arthur David (1968), is a translation of the section on the tractate *Pirqey Avot* ("Ethics of the Fathers"), an extremely important work in Maimonides' corpus. Unfortunately, the translation is based entirely on the medieval Hebrew version instead of the fine critical edition of the Judeo-Arabic text, and it is often an inaccurate rendering even of the Hebrew. Selections from it are reprinted in Twersky, *Maimonides Reader*.

The extremely important commentary on *Sanhedrin*, chapter 10 ("*Ḥeleq*") has been attempted twice in English: once by a certain "E.N." (whose identity I have been unable to discover) in the journal **Gal-Ed: Hebrew Review and Magazine of Rabbinical Literature** 1 (1835): 254-56, 283-86, 351-55. The translation is inexact and incomplete. An equally incorrect translation of Maimonides' "Thirteen Principles of Faith," which comes at the end of that introduction, appears there, pp. 398-401. The second attempt, equally bad and sometimes even worse, is by Arnold Wolf, "Maimonides on Immortality and the Principles of Judaism," **Judaism** 15 (1966): 95-101, 211-16, 337-42 (reprinted, without corrections, in Twersky, **Maimonides Reader**). I plan a correct translation of this section, based on the Arabic, in the near future.

The Eight Chapters (Shemonah Peraqim):

Actually a lengthy introduction to his commentary on *Avot* (see preceding page), this extremely important work has been critically edited and translated into English, **The Eight Chapters of Maimonides on Ethics**, by Joseph Gorfinkle (1912). Both the edition and the translation are generally sound.

"Letters," Philosophical and Other Treatises:

There is still no complete critical edition of the "Letters" and Treatises (*ma'amarim*) of Maimonides, although several have been edited in more or less acceptable fashion.

Epistle to Yemen (*Iggeret Teiman*), perhaps the most famous, dealing with philosophical and religious questions (such as the coming of the messiah, polemics, etc.), has been carefully edited and translated by Abraham Halkin and Boaz Cohen (Unfortunately Cohen did not know Arabic and so did his translation from the medieval Hebrew versions, not always making it clear even which version he used) (1952).

Millot ha-higgayon, **Maimonides' Treatise on Logic**, critical ed. and tr. Israel Efros (1938).

Letter on Astrology, tr. Ralph Lerner in Lerner and Muhsin Mahdi, **Medieval Political Philosophy** (1963; 1972), pp. 227-36 (based on critical edition of text).

Various "Letters" in **A Treasury of Jewish Letters**, ed. Franz Kobler (1954) are both incomplete and inaccurate. These are reproduced in Twersky, **Maimonides Reader**.

Guide of the Perplexed (*Moreh Nevukhim*):

There are several editions of an English translation, done from the medieval Hebrew version, by M. Friedlander (some with commentary and notes, which are still valuable, but the commonly used one-volume edition lacks these). There is also an abridged version translated by Chaim Rabin (1952). All of these are superseded by **Guide of the Perplexed**, tr. Shlomo Pines (pronounced "Pee-nus") (1963; also a paper edition). Although there are some errors in this translation, and it is lacking notes, it is based on the original Arabic text. There are important introductions by Pines and Leo Strauss. Selections of this translation (quite extensive) are reproduced in Twersky, **Maimonides Reader**, and brief selections in Lerner and Mahdi, **Medieval Political Philosophy** in their own original translation from the Arabic.

Medical Works:

Often unjustly ignored by scholars of Jewish philosophy, Maimonides' medical writings are widely admired in medical circles.

The Medical Aphorisms of Moses Maimonides, tr. Fred Rosner and Suessmann Muntner (N.Y., 1970-71; 1973; two vols.).

(Commentary on the Aphorisms of Hippocrates): introduction and commentary on First Aphorism, tr. A. Bar-Sela and H.E. Hoff, "Maimonides' Interpretation of the First Aphorism of Hippocrates," **Bulletin of the History of Medicine** 37 (1963); 347-54.

Treatise on Hemorrhoids, tr. S. Muntner and Fred Rosner (Philadelphia, 1969).

(Treatise on Poisons):

a) "Maimonides' Treatise on Poisons," tr. (from a German translation) L.J. Bragman in **Medical Journal & Record** 124(1962): 103-07,169-71.

b) Complete translation, **Treatise on Poisons and Their Antidotes**, tr. S. Muntner (Philadelphia, 1966).

Moses Maimonides' Glossary of Drug Names, tr. Fred Rosner (Philadelphia, 1979 [Memoirs of the American Philosophical Society, n.s., 54]).

Moses Maimonides' Two Treatises on the Regimen of Health, tr. (from Arabic) A. Bar-Sela, H.E. Hoff, Elias Faris (Philadelphia, 1964 [Transactions of the American Philosophical Society, n.s., 54]).

(Treatise in Elucidation of Some Accidents and the Response to it):

a) translated in preceding work;

b) **Moses Maimonides on the Causes of Symptoms**, ed. and tr. J.O. Liebowitz, *et al.* (Berkeley, 1974).

Anthologies of Translations

A Maimonides Reader, ed. Isadore Twersky (N.Y., 1972; also a paper ed.). Contains excerpts from previously published translations of many of the works indicated in the listings above (except for medical writings, none of which, strangely, merited inclusion). The translations are obviously of uneven quality, parts of the **Mishneh Torah** (from the Yale Judaica Series still under way) are more or less correct, entire chapters of Pines' translation of the **Guide** appear, and most of the rest of the translations (except for excerpts from Gorfinkle's translation of **The Eight Chapters**) are inaccurate. Nevertheless, it gives the reader unfamiliar with Hebrew or Arabic a general idea of some of Maimonides' thought.

Rambam, Readings in the Philosophy of Moses Maimonides, tr. Lenn E. Goodman (N.Y., 1976) in fact is entirely composed of selections of the **Guide**, newly translated, and one brief excerpt from **The Eight Chapters**. Some of Goodman's translations are an improvement on Pines, while others are more paraphrase than translation. Still, in some respects, the reader lacking in philosophical training may find it easier to follow Goodman's reading, and the introductory sections are often helpful.

The Teachings of Maimonides, tr. Abraham Cohen (1927; photo rpt. N.Y., 1968, with introduction by Marvin Fox). Selections arranged topically, from various works.

Maimonides, His Wisdom for Our Time, tr. Gilbert S. Rosenthal (N.Y., 1969). The best anthology, superior to anything else published. Selections include most of Maimonides' work, even some responsa. Translations are all from Hebrew, of course, but they are not bad. Sources are given only at the end of the book.

Introductory Bibliography about Maimonides

There seems no point in listing all the many books and articles, even only in English, dealing with Maimonides in general and with specific aspects of his work. However, a short list of some basic books which serve as an introduction may be useful.

Yellin, David and Israel Abrahams, **Maimonides** (Philadelphia, 1936). A basic bibliography, of some interest, but written for the popular market.

Zeitlin, Solomon. **Maimonides** (N.Y., 1935). Often overlooked today, this book still has some value.

Bratton, Fred Gladstone. **Maimonides, Medieval Modernist** (Boston, 1967). An interesting, if somewhat superficial, treatment by a sympathetic Christian.

Heschel, Abraham J. **Maimonides** (tr. from German). (N.Y., 1983).

Baron, Salo W., ed., **Essays on Maimonides** (N.Y., 1941.) Contains important and informative essays of real value.

Maimonides Octocentennial Series (N.Y., 1935). A series of important pamphlets: Ginzberg, Asher, "The Supremacy of Reason;" Marx, Alexander, "Moses Maimonides;" Tchernowitz, Chaim, "Maimonides as Codifier;" Husik, Isaac, "The Philosophy of Maimonides."

Roth, Leon. **The Guide for the Perplexed, Moses Maimonides** (N.Y., etc., 1948). Very little about the *Guide*, actually. A book for the popular market, on the general importance of Maimonides.

Twersky, Isadore. **Introduction to the Code of Maimonides** (New Haven, 1980). See my review, reprinted below in this volume.

Notes

[1] The most important study on Maimonides' biblical interpretation is Wilhelm Z. Bacher, *Die Bibelexegese Mose Maimūnis* (1896; translated also into Hebrew). Cf. also Sarah Klein-Braslavsky, *Peirush ha-Rambam le-sippur beryiat ha-ᶜolam* (1978, in Hebrew; a thorough study of his treatment of the creation story); Joseph Kafiḥ *ha-Miqra ba-Rambam* (1972, in Hebrew); J. Dienstag, "Biblical Exegesis of Maimonides in Jewish Worship," in *Samuel K. Mirsky Memorial Volume* (1970), pp. 151-90; and briefly Isadore Twersky, *Introduction to the Code of Maimonides* (1980), pp. 147-50.

[2] See the generally quite useful article of Salo Baron, "The Historical Outlook of Maimonides," American Academy for Jewish Research, *Proceedings* 6 (1935): 5-113, reprinted in his *History and Jewish Historians* (1964). The importance of the influence of Maimonides on the "founder" of the study of comparative religion has been dealt with only by Julius Guttmann, "John Spencers Erklärung der biblischen Gesetze in ihrer Beziehung zu Maimonides," *Festskrift....David Simonsens* (1923), pp. 258-76.

Maimonides' Impact on World Culture

(Commemorative Address,
Univ.of Wisconsin-Madison,
April 24, 1985)

We celebrate this year the eight hundred-and-fiftieth anniversary of the birth, on March 30, 1135, of Moses (Mūsā) ibn Maymūn, known to the world as Maimonides.

If he had been born in France or Germany, he might very well have grown up to become a great talmudic scholar, perhaps one more of those who added to the already growing body of detailed and technical legal reasoning found in the *Tosefot* (additional notes) on the Talmud. His name then would never have been known to more than a handful of rabbinic scholars throughout the ages. However, he was born instead in Córdoba in Muslim Spain, one of the greatest cities in the world, which one time had been the capital of the independent Muslim caliphate which came to an end in 1016 with the civil war which left much of the city in ruins. After that, Muslim Spain was divided into a number of provinces or city-kingdoms under more or less independent Muslim rulers. These still retained, for the most part, much of the great cultural traditions which made Spain stand out as a shining jewel in the vast Muslim world which encircled the Mediterranean.

The young Moses, born the son of a very pious and perhaps almost fanatical religious judge of the Jewish community of Córdoba, learned not only Hebrew, the Bible, and Jewish law, but also excelled in Arabic, mathematics, astronomy, Muslim and Greek philosophy, and medicine. That all of this was accomplished well before his eighteenth birthday was not at all unusual at that time. But the good fortune of his birth in such a country, at such a time, and the remarkable willingness of his father—of whom we have no evidence that he possessed any interest in secular studies—to allow his son to master these disciplines, has enabled the name of Maimonides to become universally known and respected as the greatest single genius produced by the Jewish people in all its long history.

When he was barely eleven years of age, the fanatical reactionary religious movement known as the Almohads came to power in North Africa, and within a few years also conquered most of Muslim Spain. Historians, however, have greatly exaggerated the repressiveness of this regime both with regard to secular culture within Islam and to the persecution and massacre of Christians and Jews who failed to accept the ultimatum of conversion. While they were strongly contemptuous of Christianity especially, and engaged in fierce battles against the Christians, particularly in the conquest of Lisbon in 1147, it took many years for the Almohads to consolidate their power and control of Spain. There is no evidence of real persecution of Jews until 1160, the year in which Maimonides and his family in fact left Spain and went to Fez in Morocco. That was the year in which his father wrote his famous "Letter of Consolation" concerning the increasingly intolerable situation of the Jews in these lands, and Maimonides himself in the same year wrote a letter recommending that Jews leave areas of severe persecution. The family chose Fez, as we now know, for the very good reason that there was very little persecution there.[1]

Before he left Spain, however, in his early twenties, he had already written parts of what he had planned to be a commentary on the entire Babylonian and Jerusalem Talmuds (never completed), a treatise on astronomy, and a book on logic. He had also begun, at least, his Arabic commentary on the Mishnah.

The situation finally grew worse even in Fez, and the family once again left, in 1165, for Palestine; but after only a few months, Maimonides decided to settle in Egypt, in the mostly Jewish city of Fustat near Cairo. There, his father died, and shortly afterwards his beloved brother David, a merchant in precious gems, was drowned when his ship sank in a storm near India. Maimonides then became a physician, and by this means supported himself. Later in his career, he became one of the most famous physicians in the Muslim world, and was personal doctor to the wazir (prime minister) of Egypt and his son.

There is no question that today he is best known for his great philosophical work, **Guide of the Perplexed**. Yet to understand the influence of the man and his ideas, and even correctly to understand many of the concepts in the **Guide**, we must examine his other works as well.

Consider, for example, his Arabic commentary on the Mishnah (the Mishnah was the first effort to set down in written form and in simple Hebrew the so-called "oral law," i.e., that body of tradition concerning both religious and civil law which evolved over a period of centuries in Palestine and Babylon). Not only did he provide a running summary of the laws in each tractate, he composed separate introductions to certain important parts. The most famous of these, called "Eight Chapters," is an introduction to the tractate *Pirqey Avot*, or "Ethics of the Fathers."

He begins with a discussion of the three "parts," or faculties, of the soul, and observes that the "improvement of the moral qualities is brought about by the healing of the soul and its activities...just as the physician, who endeavors to cure the human body, must have a perfect knowledge of it in its entirety and its individual parts...so he who tries to cure the soul, wishing to improve the moral qualities, must have a knowledge of the soul in its totality and its parts" and know how to maintain its health.[2]

While previous Jewish philosophers, such as Baḥya Ibn Paquda and Solomon Ibn Gabirol, had written treatises on the improvement of moral qualities, Maimonides is the first to develop a notion of what we today would call the psychological approach to health, or "holistic medicine," if you will. He recognized here, and also elsewhere in his writings, the wholeness of man and the interrelatedness of the body and the psyche.

It is in this work, in the fourth chapter, that Maimonides set forth his famous doctrine of the "golden mean." He says that virtues are "psychic conditions and dispositions which are midway between two reprehensible extremes." The way to acquire these virtues in proper balance is through constant repetition of the acts which characterize them. Thus, extremes of asceticism and self-denial are to be avoided, but rather moderation in all things is the goal.

Indeed Maimonides more than once was able to draw upon his own medical knowledge and his experience as a doctor to illustrate moral or ethical issues. Since some of these references have been ignored, by students of his philosophy or law because they are not interested in medicine, and by students of medicine because they are not familiar with his legal works, let me cite just one example. In his general introduction to the commentary on the Mishnah, he discusses the requirements for being a good judge (incidentally, he offers what I believe is a unique and quite satisfactory explanation for the apparent peculiarity that in the arrangement of the tractates of the Talmud, the treatise on ethics known as *Pirqey Avot*, "Ethics of the Fathers," is placed after *Sanhedrin* and before *Horayot*, two tractates dealing with laws concerning judges; that is because the judge must above all be concerned with ethics, he explains). There he says:

> The judge must be like an expert physician, for as long as the physician may cure by prescribing proper diet he should not use drugs, but if he sees the disease is too severe to be treated by diet then he should use drugs similar to food, such as certain kinds of drinks or mixtures of sweet spices, and if he sees that these do not prevail to cure the illness he should use stronger drugs and give the patient to drink *saqamuniah* [Arabic, derived from Greek, refers to a drug known as Convolculacaea, which is a kind of purgative] or aloes or other bitter herbs. So the judge should endeavor to resolve the matter, and if not then judge gently and speak soft words to the litigants, and if this is not possible because of the obstinacy of one of them who wants to be the victor over the other unjustly then the judge should prevail over him and make heavy his burden, as I have explained.[3]

As an example of how important Maimonides' introductions to the Mishnah are, let us turn our attention to his discussion of the allegorical interpretation and homily in the Talmud—again from his general introduction to the commentary on the Mishnah. One should not assume that these allegories are of little importance; rather, they have a very great purpose and meaning,

> for if one investigates them deeply there will be understood from them something of the absolute good than which thing is nothing higher, and there will be revealed something of metaphysical knowledge and true matters like that which men of knowledge concealed and which philosophers hid in all their generations, but when you look at them in their apparent simple meaning you will find them incomparably contrary to intelligence. They did this [concealed the true meaning] because of wondrous matters, one, to arouse the understanding of the learner, and also to close the eyes of the fools whose understanding shall never be illuminated and if the truth were unfolded before them they would turn aside from it because of the failing of their natures; concerning them it is said 'One does not reveal to them the secret' [*Qiddushin* 71a], because their intellect is not perfected to be enabled to receive the truth in certainty.

He goes on to illustrate this by the case of a certain sage of the Talmud who knew one aspect of esoteric knowledge but not another, and when he met one who was proficient in the other he suggested they exchange their knowledge. However, when he had learned what the other had to teach, he refused to reveal to him what he knew. Maimonides says he did not do this, God forbid, because of pettiness or because he wanted to appear wiser than the other, which traits would be contemptible even for ordinary people and certainly for scholars, but because he saw that he was worthy of learning and understanding what the other had to offer, but the other was not yet ready to understand what he knew. He brought as proof for this the saying, "Honey and milk under your tongue" (Song of Songs 4.11), and the explanation of the sages that this refers to the sweet senses by which enjoyment is attained, such as the taste of honey, which are concealed and not spoken of. "For these matters are not of those which it is possible to teach," Maimonides says, "and they are not explained publicly but alluded to in hidden books, and if God removes the veil from the heart of one who is found worthy before Him after he has prepared himself in the sciences [the Arabic *ᶜulūm* implies all kinds of knowledge], he will understand these things according to the power of his intellect... Thus, it is not proper for a perfect man to expound what he knows of these secrets other than to one who is greater than he or like him..."

He then goes on to explain that human intellects are divided like the division of human temperament. "There is no doubt that the intellect of one who does not know a matter is not as elevated as that of one who does know it, for the one is the active intellect and the other the potential [hylic] intellect."[4]

Interesting as all this is of itself, as well as the lengthy illustration which follows there concerning astronomical knowledge (ignored by all who have dealt with that aspect of Maimonides' work), it is also particularly relevant to what he later said concerning the limitations of intellectual apprehension, again using the comparison of esoteric knowledge to honey (but citing a different verse, Proverbs 25.16), in **Guide** I.32. Similarly, there in chapter 33, he states that one who is seen to be perfect in mind (i.e., properly prepared in study of sciences to begin metaphysical speculations) should be led step by step until he achieves complete intellectual perfection. So, he says, the true opinions in these matters were not hidden or contained in riddles by all men of knowledge (he means not only sages of the Talmud, but all the philosophers) because of anything bad in them or because they undermine the foundations of the Torah, as the ignorant people think, but because normally the intellect is incapable yet of understanding their true meaning. All of this becomes more intelligible when we have before us the earlier explanation in his commentary on the Mishnah, cited above. It might also save careless scholars who continue to talk about Maimonides' supposed intent to harmonize the apparent discrepancies between revelation and philosophy in favor of the former. This was not, in fact, his intent; rather, he maintained there were no discrepancies.

The truth manifested by revelation and the truth manifested by reason is of necessity one and the same, for there is only one truth and not, to borrow Santayana's phrase, many little truths. Revelation is for the masses, and speaks to them on the level they can understand, hiding away in riddles and parables those things for which most intellects are not prepared. The intellectually perfected man, the philosopher in short, perceives the full nature of truth. In this, as in so many other things, Maimonides shared the position of his contemporary Averroes.

In our discussion so far, we have been deliberately avoiding the **Guide**, other than casual references. This is because that work, translated into many languages (already into Latin, Hebrew and Spanish in the Middle Ages, and several others since then), is generally widely known. We wish to call attention to the other writings of Maimonides. One of these is the only work which he himself wrote in Hebrew, the **Mishneh Torah**. The title, taken from the Bible, means "repetition of the Torah." It is referred to in English usually as "Code of Jewish Law," a not altogether happy title. In Hebrew it is also known as **Yad ha-ḥazaqah**, "the Strong hand," because the numerical value of the letters of the word *Yad* is 14, and there are 14 volumes to this work. Now, a "volume" in the Middle Ages didn't always mean what we mean. We read of numerous Muslim writers who composed encyclopedic works of many "volumes" and we imagine a whole bookshelf, but are somewhat disappointed when we see the actual work and it is really quite slim. However, in this case we really mean volumes, of quite a significant size and thickness.

It would be hard to imagine any other writer in history who had composed a work of 14 large volumes which have been so ignored by the world as these have been.

In four places in his work, Maimonides has dealt with the history of the transmission of law from the Bible through the oral law to the Talmud and to his own day: in his introduction to the commentary on the Mishnah (*Zeraᶜim*), in his introduction to *Pirqey Avot*, in his introduction to the Book of Commandments **Sefer ha-Miṣvot**), and in the introduction to the code **Mishneh Torah**). Everything he says is of interest in each of these places, but this is a subject for Jewish specialists (who have largely ignored these discussions).

The first book of the **Mishneh Torah** is called "Book of Knowledge," long available in a more or less adequate English translation. It is necessary to remember that this book, like the rest of the code, was written in Hebrew, precisely (as

Maimonides tells us) so that the masses of Jews everywhere could read and understand it. Therefore, it is of more than passing interest that in the first section of this book, under the heading of "Foundations of the Torah" (not, as in the English translation, "Basic Principles of the Torah" the distinction is important, for the Hebrew term "foundations" implies matters the knowledge of which is required for every Jew) he begins with some profoundly philosophical notions.[5]

Maimonides there says: "The foundation of all foundations and the pillar of all learning is to know that there is there a First Existent and He is the cause [brings into existence] of all existing things; and all the existents in the heavens and the earth and what is between them do not exist except through the essence of his bringing into existence."[6]

He then proceeds to a discussion of contingent existence, and states that if it were to be supposed that all other things did not exist, God would still exist, for all things are in need of God, but he is not in need of them.

Now these matters are quite profound, with a long philosophical tradition going back to Aristotle. They are again taken up in great detail in the **Guide**. The question is, what are they doing here, in a code of Jewish law? We would expect a statement to the effect that it is a duty to believe that God exists, that He is one, etc. Perhaps, we might assume, if we turn to the **Book of Commandments** of Maimonides, we will find such a simple statement. We would be wrong in such an assumption. There, too, he says: "The first commandment is that which was commanded concerning the belief in the divinity, which is that we believe that there is there a Mover and Cause which activates all existents..."[7] It will be seen that there, too, the language employed is that of Aristotelian philosophy rather than biblical or even rabbinical terminology.

The solution is inescapable: Maimonides considered it imperative that even the common person have at least a fundamental understanding, not of the traditional rabbinical principles concerning God, but of the philosophical exposition of the nature of God, and he presents this as an absolute commandment and as the "foundation of all foundations" of Jewish law. This is absolutely unique in Jewish tradition, for no other codifier of law and no other of the Jewish philosophers before or after Maimonides ever stated that a knowledge of a philosophical principle was a fundamental requirement of Jewish law or belief.

It is instructive, for example, to compare what Sa^c^adyah Gaon, long before Maimonides, says concerning the belief in God: that he is one, living, omnipotent, omniscient, that nothing resembles him and that he does not resemble any of his works.[8] Now, Sa^c^adyah was opposed to Aristotelian philosophy, of course, but was strongly influenced by Neoplatonism. Still, there is nothing of that in this statement, but only the kinds of pious observations to be expected from any religious believer.

We can get even closer to the notion I am trying to convey by looking at another statement Maimonides makes in the same book, chapter two: "When a person contemplates God's great and wondrous works and creatures, he will see from them [God's] wisdom which has no limit or end, and immediately he will love" and praise God. He goes on to make clear that not only through knowledge of created things, the study of nature and all the sciences, but also the study of metaphysics, is true love of God to be achieved. Thus, we see that the acquisition of knowledge, and in all its branches, is not merely a desirable thing but an absolute commandment and obligation, without which the positive commandments of knowing God and loving God cannot be fulfilled. Ignorance is not merely a bad thing, it is a crime.

Scattered throughout the **Mishneh Torah** are similar gems of philosophical insight, and also practical and moral advice which is of lasting value. He again expounds on the "golden mean," which is repeated throughout his writings. He warns especially against pride; he cautions against flattery; and urges the virtues of silence; suggests that one should be generally cheerful. As a good doctor he says that "since keeping the body in health and perfection is of the ways of God, since it is impossible to understand or know anything of the knowledge of God if one is sick, therefore one must keep himself removed from things which harm the body and direct himself to those things which purify and make healthy," and then follows a list of very sensible suggestions on the general preservation of health, all of which I believe modern doctors would certainly agree with. Again, what is surprising here is not the advice, although it is certainly far more reasonable than much of what we find in medieval medical treatises,but that it is included in this code of law as part of the law by which the good Jew must live.

Under the category of moral advice, is there anything in any religious literature of a more noble character than this:

> The business affairs of a sage must be in truth and in faithfulness; his word is his bond [literally, saying on the no, no, and on yes, yes]. He is scrupulous with himself in his accounts, but gives and forgives when he takes from others and is not strict with them. He pays the purchase price immediately; he does not act either as surety or trustee or to assume a power of attorney [since such things lead to temptations and possible fraud]. He accepts obligation for himself in business transactions even when the Torah does not obligate him, so that he will stand by his word and not change it. If others are judged liable to him, he forgives them and loans them money and is gracious. He does not encroach on the trade of another, and does not distress a man all his life. The general rule of the matter is, he is of the persecuted but not of the persecutors, of the reviled but not the revilers.[9]

In this last remark, he is not, of course, justifying being persecuted, but saying that it would be better to be a persecuted person than to be a persecutor, etc.

We would, of course, be remiss in discussing Maimonides in not paying tribute to his great medical contributions. This is the most neglected area of research on Maimonides, and one must hunt for a few obscure articles, most of them not very good, in older issues of medical journals. Nevertheless, scholars have largely ignored his medical works, most of which have been translated and some even with quite good critical editions of the texts in Arabic and of the medieval Hebrew translations.

Maimonides was physician to the *wazīr*, or prime minister, of Egypt and then to the sultan Saladin himself. He was not, as popuar legend has it, called to be physician to Richard the Lionhearted but rather to another Christian king in Palestine, but he refused. He was unquestionably one of the most famous physicians in the entire Muslim world, second only perhaps to Ibn Zuhr of Seville, his contemporary and some say perhaps his teacher in medicine. The esteem in which he was held is evident from the earliest known biography of Maimonides by the famous Ibn Abī ᶜUṣaybiᶜah (1203-1270), himself a renowned Muslim physician and historian of medicine and an acquaintance of Maimonides' son Abraham. He wrote of Maimonides:

> *Al-Ra'is* Mūsā ibn Maymūn, the Cordovan, a Jew. He was learned in the laws of the Jews, and was counted among their learned and their sages. He was their head (*Ra'is*) in Egypt. He was unique in his time in the art of medicine and its practice, versed in the sciences and possessed of an excellent knowledge of philosophy. The sultan Al-Malik al-Nāṣir Ṣalaḥ al-Dīn (Saladin) saw and consulted him, and likewise his son al-Malik al-Afḍal ᶜAlī...

He also quotes what has become the well-known poetic praise of Maimonides by a contemporary Muslim.

> I deem Galen's medicine fit for the body alone,
> But Abū ᶜImrān's (Maimonides') for both body and mind.
> Had the medicine of the Time come to call on him,
> Through knowledge he would have cured it of ignorance's ills.
> Had the ripening moon his counsel required,
> She could attain the perfection to which she aspired.
> The day of the full moon he would cure her of spots,
> And save her from waning at the end of the month.[10]

There is a great deal in the extant medical works of Maimonides (not all has survived; he commented on sixteen books of Galen, and only fragments of the work remain) which is of more than historical interest. I well remember in my youth when an important doctor in Denver, administrator of the regional government Department of Health, told me that he found much medical information in Maimonides which was remarkably ahead of its time and in line with the most modern theories. I have since heard this repeatedly.

He was a firm believer in proper diet. In his **Regimen of Health**, he again warns about this and advises eating less in hot weather than in cold. He adds: "If man were to conduct himself as he manages the animal he rides, he would be safeguarded from many ailments." Man uses judgement in feeding his animal, yet he himself eats indiscriminately, without measure. Furthermore, he takes care to exercise his animal, but pays no attention to the exercise of his own body, "which is the cornerstone of the conservation of health and the repulsion of most ailments." He urges precisely the kind of aerobic exercise which is recommended today: vigorous, rapid motion "in which the respiration alters and one begins to heave sighs." We must recall that it is only in quite recent time that physicians have begun to realize the importance of exercise of this kind. Among foods he advises are only whole wheat bread made of coarse, unrefined flour; sheep not more than two years old, but without fat; fowl, which is preferable to beef; milk if it can be tolerated, but no cheese; small fish of white flesh in moderation; and wine, which he repeatedly praises as very beneficial (except that elsewhere he says adolescents should not use it at all because it corrupts their bodies and their souls). Nevertheless, he was generally against vegetables and fruits, other than for medicinal purposes, a fact which is particularly strange since Jews and Muslims, especially in Spain, ate almost every fruit and vegetable known to us today. This apparent aversion is due to Galen, whom he quotes as being completely opposed to the eating of fruit.

Like a good Jew, he prescribes chicken soup—well, actually a lemon broth made with a fat hen, "much carthamus [a kind of herb], sugar, lemon juice, and beets." (Matzoh balls are not mentioned in the recipe!)

He again shows a strong interest, in this and elsewhere in his medical writings, in psychology, observing that "the passions of the psyche produce changes in the body," and thus physicians should always give attention to the balance of the psychic state of health as well as the physical.

In another medical treatise, written for the son of Saladin, he prescribes again proper diet (this time including certain fruits and vegetables, but never peaches), daily exercise, proper rest in pleasant surroundings (not many of us can afford to hire servants to play soothing music on stringed instruments as we go to sleep, as he advised the ruler's son, but perhaps Maimonides would have approved of modern stereos as long as rock music is banished from them; not for Jews, however, for Maimonides has a famous legal responsum in which he prohibits listening to any kind of music since we are in mourning for the Temple).

His medical works are an indication of the extent to which he was centuries ahead of his time not only in his abilities in diagnosis and treatment, but also in such modern concerns as the dangers of pollution, both of air and water and the environment in general. We only have to read what he says of the pollution of the air in the cities of his day due to the high buildings, narrow streets, dead animals, and refuse of all kinds, and his very practical advice about living where pollution is minimal, or at least in a house with broad open courtyards where the sun and wind can cleanse the air, to realize that life in a medieval city was not necessarily more pleasant than in today's cities.

His concern, as we have said, was for the total health of the individual. Many a modern physician might wish to have on his wall, rather than the spurious "Prayer of the Physician" long attributed to Maimonides, these authentic words:

> Concern and care should always be given to the movements of the psyche; these should be kept in balance in the state of health as well as in disease, and no other regimen should be given precedence in any wise. The physician should make every effort that all the sick, and all the healthy, should be most cheerful of soul at all times, and that they should be relieved of the passions of the psyche that cause anxiety.[11]

We have not discussed Maimonides' *magnum opus*, the **Guide of the Perplexed**, except in passing. This is a monumental work, the proper understanding of which requires a complex background of Greek and Muslim philosophy, science and religion, law and philology. Even to begin to go into these matters in such a paper as this would be impossible. It is, however, a sad comment on the state of Maimonidean scholarship that we still have no adequate notes or commentary on this work.

What is of interest for our present discussion is to point out the influence which this work had on the entire history of Christian philosophy in the Middle Ages, and afterwards on such philosophers as Leibniz, who wrote an interesting commentary on the Latin translation of the **Guide** made by the great Christian Hebraist Johannes Buxtorf, *fil*, and Spinoza, who utilized that same translation. Among the Christian Scholastics who utilized the **Guide**, some favorably and some quite critically, were Albertus Magnus, Robert Grosseteste, Alexander of Hales, St. Thomas Aquinas, and many others. Maimonides is severely criticized, strictly for not being in accord with official Catholic doctrine, by Giles of Rome (incidentally, the edition and English translation of his *Errors of the Philosophers* published by Marquette University in Milwaukee contains some extremely valuable information on the translation of Maimonides utilized by Giles; by contrast, the superficial and almost condescending treatment of Maimonides in the introduction to the texts of St. Thomas, Siger of Brabant, and St. Bonaventure *On the Eternity of the World*, also done by Marquette, is unfortunate). Many scholars have discussed these matters in detail in various articles and books, and these matters are mostly for the specialists in these respective philosophers.

Obviously, then, the influence of Maimonides in the Christian world was profound, lasting long beyond the medieval period. While other Jewish thinkers, such as Philo, Isaac Israeli and Ibn Gabirol, also left their influence on medieval Christian thought, none had the lasting impact of Maimonides. There were other areas of this influence as well, which have scarcely been investigated yet, such as the area of the comparative study of religions, beginning in the seventeenth century and due almost entirely to Maimonides' discussion in the **Guide**. There is also no question but that Maimonides had a considerable influence on the work of the great English Hebraist and scholar of law, John Selden, also of the seventeenth century. The extent of his possible influence on the entire Christian Hebraist movement has not, as far as I am aware, even been considered.

We should also note his impact on later developments in Jewish philosophy. Philo was completely unknown to the medieval Jewish world, and Ibn Gabirol's work was too obscure and too Neo-platonic to have any impact whatsoever, so that both these Jewish philosophers were far more influential in Christian than in Jewish thought. Without Maimonides, therefore, there hardly would have been such a thing as Jewish philosophy. All of the philosophical writers who came after him, chiefly in medieval Spain but also in Provence and Italy, were more or less commentators on his thought. What this means for world culture is not entirely clear, but certainly it broadened the horizons and outlook of the Jewish world. After the Renaissance, however, Maimonides as a philosopher fell under a cloud of complete and deliberate obscurity in the Jewish world until the end of the eighteenth century when Moses Mendelssohn studied him and led the way for the development of the Jewish Englightenment.

What we can admire most about Maimonides today, I believe, is his rigorous and systematic devotion to the principles of balance and harmony, the pursuit of the "golden mean," for which he is so famous, in all areas of life: physical and psychic well-being, philosophy and faith, morality and enjoyment of life, etc. Equally rigorous was the principle which guided him in all of his work and throughout his life, absolute devotion to truth and knowledge.

And so we might best conclude this discussion by citing two or three of Maimonides' own statements in this regard:

> Do not consider a thing proof because you find it written in books; for just as a liar will deceive with his tongue, he will not be deterred from doing the same thing with his pen. They are utter fools who accept a thing as convincing proof because it is in writing. The truth of a thing does not become greater by its frequent repetition, nor is it lessened by lack of repetition.

> Let the truth and right by which you are apparently the loser be preferable to you to the falsehood and wrong by which you are apparently the gainer.[12]

So we salute Moses ben Maimon of Córdoba, the Jew, on this 850th anniversary of his birth.

Maimonides and the Non-Jewish World In the Middle Ages

Since Maimonides was, without question, the most original and the most important of all Jewish scholars (at least of the medieval period, and possibly without even that qualification), it is not surprising that his thought and work had a profound influence also on the non-Jewish world.

So much bad history has been written about the relationships of Jews and Muslims in the Middle Ages, to say nothing of Jewish-Christian relations, that what Baron has aptly termed the lachrymose conception of Jewish history may blind us to the reality that Jews and Gentiles could often appreciate each other and even learn from each other (this will be fully investigated, with regard to medieval Spain, in my forthcoming book on this subject). Maimonides, too, received the adulation of Muslim scholars, and not only for his medical work where his reputation as the foremost authority in the field was well-established in his own lifetime. (The statement of Ibn Abī ᶜUṣaybᶜiah on Maimonides as a physician has been quoted above at length; none of this is mentioned, nor any of the other Muslim sources dealing with Maimonides, in the recent superficial book of Bernard Lewis, who even continues to give credence to the long disproved myth of Maimonides' "conversion" to Islam.[13])

According to the account of a nearly contemporary Muslim writer, a Ṣūfī by the name of Abū ᶜAlī Ibn Hūd, born in Murcia and the son of the Muslim governor there (born in 1235) and thus a member of the famous Banū Hūd family of Spain, went to Damascus and there was responsible for urging *Jews* to study the **Guide**![14]

Obviously, there were already manuscripts of the *Guide* available in Arabic characters shortly after the death of Maimonides, and perhaps even earlier. There is still extant a fifteenth-century Arabic manuscript of the **Guide** (perhaps there are others; I have not examined the many catalogues, nor has anyone else as far as I know). There is also an even earlier Muslim commentary on the "Book of Knowledge" (*Sefer ha-Mada*^{c}) of the **Mishneh Torah**.[15] This fact provides further evidence of the significant knowledge of Hebrew among Muslim scholars in medieval Spain, which will be detailed in my aforementioned book.

Turning to the Christian world, it is not surprising that a considerable amount of attention has been given to the influence of Maimonides on St. Thomas Aquinas, both by Christian and Jewish scholars. However, the impact of Maimonides on Scholasticism by no means is limited to Aquinas. Numerous medieval Christian writers made use of the **Guide**, usually critically, but sometimes derived some positive light from it as well. Translations of the **Guide**, first in Spanish and then frequently in Latin and even Italian, and the medieval and Renaissance Latin translations of the **Mishneh Torah**, helped spread knowledge of his ideas also to the Christian world.[16]

There is one more area to be mentioned when discussing the impact of Maimonides on the Christian world of the Middle Ages, and that is yet another myth which continues to persist in spite of the fact that there is absolutely no solid evidence. This is that "the Church," or specifically the Dominicans, were responsible for the burning of the **Guide** which supposedly took place in Montpellier. At the time, 1232, the Dominicans were primarily concerned with the Albigensian and other Christian heresies, and certainly had not yet turned their attention to the Jews (in fact, other than persistent and admittedly unpleasant attempts to convert the Jews, the Dominicans did not punish Jews as such in any way at all; their own jurisdiction was over

Christian heretics, and of course Jewish *conversos* in Spain who were accused—usually falsely—of being heretics). In fact, the **Guide** served as fuel against the Albigensian heresy in at least one medieval Christian tract, and whether or not it also was "fuel" in a literal sense in Montpellier, the Church had nothing to do with it.[17]

Maimonides and Scholasticism

The general medievalist, as well as those interested in medieval philosophy and theology, may find useful this specialized bibliography of studies dealing specifically with the impact of Maimonides on medieval Scholasticism. Recently there appeared a volume of reprints of some of the articles dealing with Maimonides and Aquinas (No. 9 below). A bibliography on Maimonides and Aquinas appears there, pp. 334-45. Necessarily, some of that will be duplicated here (although there are misspellings and omissions in that list). Excluded here are references, usually brief and vague, in standard works on medieval philosophy.

1. Baeumker, Clemens. "Über die Philosophie der europäischen Völker im Mittelalter, 1897-1907," *Archiv für Geschichte der Philosophie* 22 (1909): 132-34 (rpt. in No. 9).

2. Blumberg, Harry. "The Problem of Immortality in Avicenna, Maimonides and St. Thomas Aquinas," *Harry Austryn Wolfson Jubilee Volume* (Jerusalem, 1965) I, 165-285 (rpt. in No. 9).

3. __________ "The separate intellects in the teaching of Maimonides" (Hebrew, with English summary), *Tarbiz* 40 (1971): 216-25.

4. Brüngel, Ferdinand, "Maimonides' Agnosticism and Scholasticism," Central Conference of American Rabbis. *Journal* 19 (1972): 65-68 (rpt. in No. 9).

5. Brunner, Peter. *Problem der Teleologie bei Maimonides, Thomas von Aquin und Spinoza* (Heidelberg, 1928).

6. Casciaro, José María. *El dialogo de Santo Tomás con musulmanes y judíos; el tema de la profecía y la revelacióon* (Madrid, 1960).

7. Dales, R.C. "Maimonides and Boethius of Daeia on the Eternity of the World," *New Scholasticism* 56 (1982): 306-19.

8. Dienstag, Jacob. "Christian Translations of Maimonides' *Mishneh Torah*," *Salo W. Baron Jubilee Volume*, ed. Saul Lieberman (Jerusalem, 1974) I, 287-309.

9. _________ ed. *Studies in Maimonides and St. Thomas Aquinas* (N.Y., 1975).

10. Fakhry, Majid. "The 'Antinomy' of the Eternity of the World in Averroes, Maimonides and Aquinas," *Le Museon* 66 (1953): 139-55 (rpt. in No. 9).

11. Feldman, Seymour. "A Scholastic Misinterpretation of Maimonides' Doctrine of Divine Attributes," *Journal of Jewish Studies* 19 (1968): 23-29 (rpt. in No. 9).

12. _________ "Did the Scholastics Have an Accurate Knowledge of Maimonides?" *Studies in Medieval Culture* 3 (1970): 145-50.

13. Fox, Marvin, "Maimonides and Aquinas on Natural Law," *Dinei Yisrael* 3 (1972): v-xxxvi (English section) (rpt. in No. 9).

14. Funkenstein, Amos. "Gesetze und Geschichte zur historisierenden Hermeneutik bei Moses Maimonides und Thomas von Aquin," *Viator* 1 (1970): 147-78 (important article; strangely not rpt. in No. 9).

15. Gilson, Etienne. "Maimonides et la philosophie de l'Exode," *Mediaeval Studies* 13 (1951): 223-25 (rpt. in No. 9).

16. Guttmann, Jacob. "Der Einfluss der maimonischen Philosophie auf das christliche Abendland," in W. Bacher, *et al.*, *Moses ben Maimon* (Leipzig, 1908) I, 153-230 (partial rpt. in No. 9).

17. _________ *Die Scholastik des 13. Jahrhunderts in ehren Beziehungen zum Judentum und jüdischer Literatur* (Breslau, 1902), pp. 85-120.

18. _________ *Das Verhältnis Thomas von Aquino zum Judentum* (Göttingen, 1891).

19. ________ "Guilllaume d'Auvergne et la litterature juive," *Révue des études juives* 18 (1889): 243-55.

20. ________ "Alexandre de Hales et le judaisme," *ibid.* 19 (1889): 224-31.

21. Harasta, Koloman. "Die Bedeutung Maimunis für Thomas von Aquin," *Judaica* (Zurich) 2 (1955): 65-83 (rpt. in No. 9).

22. Husik, Isaac. "An Anonymous Medieval Christian Critic of Maimonides," *Jewish Quarterly Review* (n.s.) 2 (1911): 159-90.

23. Joël, Manuel. "Etwas über den Einfluss der jüdischen Philosophie auf die christliche Scholastik," *Monatsschrift für Geschichte und Wissenschaft des Judentums* 9 (1860): 207-17, 284.

24. ________ *Das Verhältnis Albert der Grossen zu Moses Maimonides* (Breslau, 1876; photo rpt. Merrick, N.Y., 197-?).

25. Kaufmann, David. "Der Führer Maimunis in der Weltliteratur," *Archiv für Geschichte der Philosophie* 9 (1898): 335-76; rpt. in his *Gesammelte Schriften* (Frankfurt a. M., 1910) II, 152-89.

26. Koplowitz, Ernest S. *Über die Abhängigkeit Thomas von Aquins von Boethius und von Mose ben Maimon* (Kallmünz, 1935; photo rpt. Merrick, N.Y., 197-?).

27. Kluxen, W. "Maimonides und die Hochscholastik," *Philosophisches Jahrbuch* 63 (1954): 151-64.

28. ________ "Literargeschichtliches zum lateinischen Moses Maimonides," *Recherches de théologie ancienne et médiévale* 21 (1951): 23-50.

29. Liebeschütz, Hans. "Judaism and Jewry in the Social Doctrine of Thomas Aquinas," *Journal of Jewish Studies* 13 (1962): 57-81 (rpt. in No. 9).

30. Levinger, J. Lee. "The Influence of Maimonides on Scholastic Thought," *Jews in the Arts and Sciences* (Jubilee volume of the Jewish [*not* Israel] Academy of Arts and Sciences [??], 1954), pp. 99-103.

31. Miller, C.L. "Maimonides and Aquinas on Naming God," *Journal of Jewish Studies* 28 (1977): 65-71.

32. Nirenstein, Samuel. *The Problem of the Existence of God in Maimonides, Alanus and Averroes* (Philadelphia, 1924). An abstract from this very important book appeared under the same title in *Jewish Quarterly Review* (n.s.) 14: 395-454.

33. Riedl, John O. "Maimonides and Scholasticism," *New Scholasticism* 10 (1936): 18-29.

34. Rohner, Anselm. *Das Schöpfungsproblem bei Moses Maimonides, Albertus Magnus und Thomas von Aquin* (Münster, 1913).

35. Singer, Charles. "The Jewish Factor in Medieval Thought," in E.R. Bevan and C. Singer, *The Legacy of Israel* (Oxford, 1927), especially pp. 251-71 (partial rpt. in No. 9).

36. Smalley, Beryl. "William of Auvergne, John of la Rochelle and St. Thomas Aquinas on the Old Law," *Aquinas Commemorative Studies* (Toronto, 1974) II, 11-73.

37. Teicher, J.L. "Christian Theology and Jewish Opposition to Maimonides," *Journal of Theological Studies* 43 (1942): 68-76.

38. Vansteenbistein, P.C. "Autori arabi e giudei nell'opera di San Tomaso," *Angelicum* 25 (1960): 336-41 (especially pp. 374-94).

39. Wolfson, Harry A. "The Kalam Arguments for Creation in Saadia, Averroes, Maimonides and St. Thomas," *Saadia Anniversary Volume* (N.Y., 1943), pp. 197-245.

40. ________ "The Meaning of Ex Nihilo in the Church Fathers, Arabic and Hebrew Philosophy, and St. Thomas," *Mediaeval Studies in Honor of Jeremiah Denis Matthias Ford* (Cambridge, Mass., 1948), pp. 355- 70; rpt. in Wolfson, *Studies in the History of Philosophy and Religion* (Cambridge, Mass., 1973) I, 207-21.

41. ________ "Nicholas of Autrecourt and Ghazali's Argument Against Causality," *Speculum* 44 (1969): 234-38.

To date, these are all of the studies dealing with the impact of Maimonides on Scholasticism, as far as I know. I should appreciate being informed of any oversights or new works. Please note that almost all of these are available at the University of Wisconsin library.

Notes

[1] Details on the Almohad conquest of Spain and the Jews will be in my book on Jewish, Muslim and Christian relations in medieval Spain. The most important article on the Almohad policy towards Jews and Christians in North Africa, correcting many earlier misconceptions, is David Corcos-Abulafia, "The nature of the relationship of the Almohad rulers to the Jews" (Hebrew, with English summary, p. ii) in *Zion* (*Ṣiyyon*) 32(1967): 137-60.

[2] **The Eight Chapters of Maimonides on Ethics**, ed. and tr. Joseph Gorfinkle (N.Y., 1912), p. 38 (tr.).

[3] **Mishnah ᶜim perirush Mosheh b. Maimon**, ed. (Judeo-Arabic) and tr. (Hebrew) Joseph Kafiḥ (Jerusalem, 1963), introduction to *Zeraᶜim* (Vol. 1), p. 30. For a brief discussion of Maimonides' statements concerning the qualities of judges in his code of law (**Mishneh Torah, Mishpaṭim, "Sanhedrin,"** 2.1-7), see Isadore Twersky, *Introduction to the Code of Maimonides* (New Haven, 1980), p. 147 (it is unfortunate that Twersky did not cite also this statement from the Mishnah commentary for comparison).

[4] *Mishnah*, ibid., pp. 35-37 (*ᶜaql bi-al-qūwa*); cf. **Guide** I.68 (p. 165).

[5] On the "Book of Knowledge," see Kraemer's article cited in the paper (below) "Maimonides and Some Muslim Sources" at n. 3. His expectation there (p. 126, n. 28) that Twersky would deal with this book, or indeed that he would provide a systematic discussion of the contents of the code of law, in his *Introduction to the Code of Maimonides*, was unfortunately not realized. Twersky's long and mostly irrelevant chapter "Law and Philosophy" is disappointing and hardly refers to "Book of Knowledge."

[6] **Mishneh Torah, Sefer ha-madaᶜ, "Yesodey ha-Torah"** (Book of Knowledge, "Foundations of the Torah") I.1 (this is my translation, for all the English translations are wrong and misleading here)

[7] **"Sefer ha-miṣvot ᶜaseh"** 1 ("Positive commandments" 1;

again my translation. The text is readily available, e.g., ed. Joseph Kafiḥ (Jerusalem, 1958); ed. Charles Chavel (Jerusalem, 1980). For English translations, see my introductory essay here, "Introducing Maimonides to the English Reader.")

[8] *Book of Beliefs and Opinions*, tr. Samuel Rosenblatt (New Haven, 1948), p. 94.

[9] **Mishneh Torah, Sefer ha-mada^c, "De^cot"** 5.13.

[10] **^cUyūn al-anabā' fī ṭabaqāt al-atibbā'**, ed. A. Müller (Königsberg, 1884) II, 117-18; tr. in Moses b. Maimon, **Two Treatises on the Regimen of Health**, ed. and tr. A. Bar-Sela, H. Hoff, E. Faris (Philadelphia, 1964 [Transactions of the American Philosophical Society, N.S. 54, pt. 4]), pp. 3-4, including the poem.

[11] Moses b. Maimon, **Two Treatises on the Regimen of Health**, p. 27.

[12] Various aphorisms, quoted in Fred Gladstone Bratton, *Maimonides, Medieval Modernist* (Boston, 1967), p. 111; and by Victor Goodhill, "Maimonides—Modern Medical Relevance," American Academy of Ophtalmology and Otolaryngology. *Transactions* 75 (2) (1971): 485 (the article, pp. 473-91, is the best on this aspect of Maimonides' work).

[13] *The Jews of Islam* (Princeton, 1984), see p. 100 (citing a source known to be extremely biased and unreliable). This is altogether a disappointing book coming from a respected scholar who has elsewhere contributed much to our knowledge of Islam.

[14] See the account by Ignaz Goldziher in *Jewish Quarterly Review* (o.s.) 6 (1894): 218-20; rpt. in his *Gesammelte Schriften* (Hildesheim, 1969) III, 319-21.

[15] The ms. of the **Guide** in Arabic described by Franz Rosenthal in *Journal of the American Oriental Society* 75: 20 (No. XVI). Muslim commentary on the "Book of Knowledge," partially edited and translated by G. Margoliouth in *Jewish Quarterly Review* (o.s.) 13 (1900-01): 488-507. This was unknown to Twersky, *Introduction to the Code of Maimonides*.

[16] On the Latin versions of the **Guide**, see the very important articles of Kluxen in the bibliography below, and for the **Mishneh Torah**, Dienstag (No. 8 in the bibliography below).

[17] The myth of the burning of the **Guide** appears often in Jewish "history" (cf., e.g., William Popper, *The Censorship of Hebrew Books* [1899; photo rpt. N.Y., 1969] p. 7. Fortunately, Daniel Jeremy Silver, *Maimonidean Criticism and the Maimonidean Controversy* (Leiden, 1969), pp. 152-53, gives a less gullible account, but does not go far enough. There is a need for a completely new and accurate treatment of the controversy by a competent historian (Silver's book is full of errors, only a few of which were noted by G. Vajda in his review in *Révue des études juives* 125: 432-36). For the citation of the **Guide** in the anti-Albigensian tract of Moneta of Cremona (a Dominican!) in 1240, shortly after the Dominicans are supposed to have burned the *Guide*, see Kluxen, "Literargeschichtliches...zu Maimonides" (No. 28 in the bibliography above), p. 33. On the subject of Albigensians and the Jews generally, disproving supposed Jewish "influences" on the Christian heresy and vice-versa, see my "Jews and Albigensians in the Middle Ages: Lucas of Túy on heretics in Leon," *Sefarad* 41 (1981): 71-93.

Maimonides—Some New Translations

Some very important statements in the work of Maimonides either have never been translated into English, or have been incorrectly translated. Even where there is a basically correct translation, for instance, of the Introduction to the Commentary on the Mishnah, it has been made on the basis of a medieval Hebrew translation and not from the original Arabic text. Precisely those passages which deal with important philosophical concepts are therefore most often incorrectly translated. A mere paraphrase will not do when dealing with Maimonides, whose thought was precise and clear on every subject.

Therefore, this section contains a selection of statements by Maimonides on matters which may be most of interest to general readers (i.e., not dealing exclusively with Jewish law or concepts). Although every effort has been made to give a correct and accurate translation, sometimes sacrificing beauty of style in the effort, and to locate sources in philosophical, biblical and rabbinical texts, the result here should be considered a "first draft" of the translations which needs much polishing before a complete version could be made.

I have divided the selections into categories or topics, labeling them accordingly. Footnotes are at the end of the chapter.

Prophecy

Know that prophecy does not help in the interpretation of the Torah and the learning of the laws [Arabic *furū*^{c}; branches, subdivisions; but ^{c}*ilm al-furū*^{c}, applied law] by the thirteen principles [rules by which scriptural law is deduced]; rather, what Joshua and Pinhas did in investigation and analogy [after the death of Moses] is also what Rabina and Rav Ashiy did [redactors of the Talmud]. But the advantage of the prophet and his actions in the Law is of the great and mighty foundations upon which the religion rests, as my soul lives!

It appears to me desirable to explan this foundation, and this is not possible except after dealing [*taqsīm*] with the claim of the prophet to prophecy, since this is also a great principle in which the masses of people and also some of the educated ones have erred [e.g., Saᶜadyah Gaon; cf. *Book of Beliefs and Opinions*, III. 4]. This is that they think that prophecy is not verified until he performs a miracle like the miracles of Moses and changes the course of nature, as did Elijah who resurrected the son of the widow [I Kings 17], or, as is known to all, like the miracles of Elisha. This principle is not correct, since all the signs which Elijah and Elisha and others of the prophets did were not done to verify their prophecy, which was already verified before this, but rather because they needed them [there was a necessity at that time to perform a miracle]; and because of their closeness to God, he fulfilled their desire, as the righteous were promised 'You shall decree a thing and it shall be established for you' [Job 22.28]...(*There follows a discussion first of false prophets, who prophesy in the name of idolatry; then he turns to the true prophet)*:

Also he who prophesies in the name of God falls into two categories:

The first category is one who prophesies in the name of God and calls and admonishes [people] to His worship and says that God added a commandment to the commandment or deleted a commandment from all the commandments included in the Torah; and there is no difference whether he adds or deletes in the scriptural commandments, or in the accepted interpretation (*here follow examples*)...such a one also shall die by strangulation [Deut. 13.6] since he is a false prophet and attributed to God what He did not tell him. Also in this case, one does not worry about a sign or miracles, since the Prophet [Moses] who amazed all the world with his miracles and God placed in our hearts his veracity and faith in him...already informed us by the word of God that there will not come from God any Torah other than this one [Deut. 30.12]...Therefore the sages, of blessed memory, said 'No prophet has permission to innovate [a law] hereafter' [*Megillah* 2b]...

The second category is one who calls [people] to the worship of God and admonishes them about his Torah, and commands them to observe the Torah without additions or deletions...and promises benefits to those who observe it and punishment to those who transgress it, as Isaiah, Jeremiah, Ezekiel and others did. He commands commandments and gives warnings which are not in matters of religion, for instance: 'Make war against such and such a town or people now,' as Samuel commanded Saul to make war with Amalek [I Samuel 15.3]. Or he admonishes not to kill, as Elisha warned Yehoram not to kill the soldiers of Hazael [king of Syria] found in Samaria, as is known [II Kings 6.22]... Therefore, when a prophet claims prohecy and does not ascribe it to idolatry and does not add to the words of Torah or delete from them, rather engages in other things as we have explained, we must examine him in order to verify his claim; if his words are verified, we are obligated to listen to all which he commands, from the minutest to the greatest of matters, and he who transgresses anything of what he commands is guilty of death at the hands of heaven [i.e., God will punish him, not the court]...but if his prophecy is not verified, his [the false prophet's] death is by strangulation.

Prophecy is verified as I shall state; when he claims to prophesy as we have described, and he is worthy of it, that is, he is of the learned and religious people [*min ahl al-ᶜilm wa'l-dīn*], morally pure [or, perhaps, chaste], intelligent, and with all the good qualities of character, according to the rule we have that prophecy does not rest except on one who is wise, powerful and rich [*Shabbat* 92a; powerful in conquering his desires, rich in being content with his lot]. There are many details in this matter which are impossible now to enumerate, and discussion of them and the proofs of each of them from scripture and from the words of the sages and other things would be a book in itself—and maybe God will help with it in what is necessary to compose on this matter. (*He thus alludes to his intention to compose a separate book on prophecy, to which he referred too in the introduction to* **Guide**, p. 9.)

If he is fit for [prophecy] as is necessary and says that he prophesies, we say to him: Make us promises and inform us what God has informed you, and he says [them]; if all his promises are fulfilled we know the veracity of his prophecy, and if he lies in something of his words, even the least of them, then we know that he has lied...Also if his words are fulfilled in one or two promises, his prophecy is not absolutely verified by this, but it remains with us suspended until there results the veracity of all which he speaks in the name of God time after time, and therefore it is said of Samuel when it was known and verified that all he said was fulfilled, 'And all Israel from Dan to Beersheba knew that Samuel was truly a prophet of the Lord' [I Samuel 3.20].

In all their affairs they asked the prophets, and if they had not asked the prophets about all their affairs Saul would not have gone to ask Samuel about the loss he sustained at the beginning [of the story; I Samuel 3.9]. Without doubt the thing is thus, since God raised up for us prophets for all requests in place of the seers of the stars, the enchanters and diviners, that we should ask them in all our affairs generally and par ticularly. And they will inform us of correct answers by the word of God; just as those diviners announce things that sometimes are fulfilled and sometimes are not ... Therefore, they called a prophet 'seer' because he sees future things before they happen [I Samuel 9.9].

(Translated from the Arabic text and Hebrew translation of Joseph Kafiḥ, **Misnah ᶜim peirush rabbeinu Mosheh ben Maimon** [Jerusalem, 1963] I, 4-8; cf. also the English translation from the Hebrew only by Fred Rosner, tr., **Moses Maimonides' Commentary on the Mishnah. Introduction to Seder Zeraim and Commentary on Tractate Berachoth** [N.Y., 1975], pp. 44-52. It is important to compare the above section from the Introduction to the Mishnah with the similar discussion about prophecy in **Guide** II. 32; a difficult passage which does not mean all that it appears to mean, about which I plan to write elsewhere).

The Purpose of Man

When we have found that the end of all [that exists] is the existence of man (i.e., man is the purpose, or final end, for which all else exists), it is an obligation to investigate also why man exists and what is his end (purpose). And when they (scholars) investigate deeply into this, they found that man has very many activities, whereas all the species of life and trees possess only one activity or two, and one end; as we see that the palm tree has no other activity than to produce dates, and so with the rest of the trees. And so with animals, there is among them a weaver, such as the spider, and a builder, like the *sunūnū* [a kind of swallow], or a gatherer like the leopard (*originally the text read: "hunter like the lions," but Maimonides himself made the correction; according to Kafiḥ's note).* But man has many activities, and therefore they investigated deeply all his activities one by one in order to know what is his purpose from all these activities, and they found that it is one single activity and the rest are only to insure his survival in order to perfect that unique activity, which is comprehension of the intelligibles and knowledge of the essences as they actually are. For it is impossible that the end of man should be to eat or drink or copulate or build a house or be a king, since all these are accidents which happen to him and do not add to his essence [existence].[1] Further, all these activities are shared by him with the rest of living creatures, and wisdom [*ᶜilm*] is what adds to his essence and transfers him from a low [or reprehensible; dh*amīma*] state to an exalted [*rafī*ᶜ state, because he was man in potentiality and has become man in actuality; for man before he has learned (acquired knowledge) is only like an animal, for man is not differentiated from other animals except by the ability to reason, in that he is a rational animal—I mean by the word 'reason' the apprehension of intelligibles, and the greatest of these is the apprehension of the unity of God, mighty and exalted, and all that is connected to it in metaphysics; for the rest of knowledge [the sciences] is only a preparation for metaphysics, and a complete discussion of this would be very lengthy. But with the apprehension of the intelligibles is necessary a repudiation of excess [*iṭṭirāḥ al-ifrāṭ]* in bodily pleasures, for the beginning of intellect (brings) the apprehension that the destruction of the soul is the fitness [*ṣalāḥ*] of the body and the fitness of the soul is the destruction of the body.[2] For if man pursues desires and arouses the senses and makes his intellect subservient to his desires and becomes like animals and ostriches who have nothing in their imagination other than eating, drinking, and copulating, then there is not recognizable in him the divine potential—that is, the intellect, and then he will be like separated matter floating in the primeaval sea [*baḥr al-hayūlī]*.

It is clear from all these introductory remarks that the purpose (of man) in this world and of all that is in it is (to be) and excellent (good) learned man, and when a man has acquired knowledge and deeds [*al-ᶜilm wa'l-ᶜamal*]—I mean by 'knowledge' apprehension of the essences as they actually are and the comprehension of all that it is possible for man to comprehend, and by 'deeds'an equilibrium in matters of (his) nature and not be addicted to them (the Arabic is unclear) and not to take from them (physical pleasures) other than what is necessary for the survival of the body, and so with the improvement of all the qualities; and man in this state is the goal (of creation).

And this thing is not known only from the prophets; also the sages of previous communities (nations), even though they did not see the prophets nor hear their words, already knew that man is not perfect unless he combines knowledge and deeds. Let it suffice for you the words of the greatest of the philosophers: 'the goal of God for us is that we be discerning and righteous.'[3] For if man were wise and understanding but pursuing pleasures, he is not truly wise, for the beginning of wisdom is not to take of the physical pleasures except (what is necessary) for the survival of the body, and in our commentary to *Pirqey Avot* we will complete this matter and explain it as is desirable...

There remains here one question, and it is that it is possible to ask: You have already said that divine wisdom has not produced anything in vain, and that of all created things in the sublunary sphere man is the most noble, and that the purpose of the human species is the apprehension of the intelligibles; if so, why has God created people who do not apprehend the intelligible, for we see that the majority of people are empty of wisdom and pursuing pleasures, and the learned and pure man is alone and strange—there are only found individuals in each generation.

The answer is that the existence of all these created beings is for two reasons; one, to serve that (unique) individual, for if all people were learned and philosophizing, the world would be lost and man destroyed from it in a short while, for man is greatly lacking and in need of many things and it would be necessary for him to learn harvesting and sowing, threshing and grinding and cooking and making tools for all this in order to obtain food, and so he would need to learn spinning and weaving in order to weave something to wear, and construction to build for himself a shelter, and to make tools for all these, and the life of Methuselah [*who lived 969 years*; Genesis 5.26-27] would not suffice to learn all the crafts that man absolutely needs in order to survive. And if so, when will he learn wisdom and understand knowledge? Therefore, all these (other people) are found in order to perform these labors which the world needs, and the learned man exists for himself, and thus is the world built and wisdom found; and how lovely is the proverb which says: 'Were it not for fools, the world would be destroyed.'[4] There is no greater foolishness than this that man weak of soul and of bodily constitution travels from the ends of the second climate to the ends of the sixth[5], and crosses seas in the days of winter and deserts in the burning heat of summer, and endangers himself to various species of predatory beasts, in order that perhaps he may earn a dollar. And when he collects all that money for which he has given all his soul, he gives it to craftsmen to build for him a solid foundation with lime and stones on virgin earth in order to erect a building that will stand hundreds of years, and he knows for a fact that there does not remain of his life even enough to consume (dwell in) a building of reeds [*bardī*]. Is there a greater stupidity than this? So all the pleasures of the world and its delights are stupidity so that the world may be built (may function), and therefore our sages, peace to them, called one who has not learned: *ᶜam ha-areṣ* [literally, *'people of the earth'*]; that is, that he was not created except for the building of the earth, and therefore is he associated with it.

(Introduction to Commentary on the Mishnah, as in the preceding selection; ed. Kafiḥ, pp. 41-44; cf. translation of Rosner, pp. 123-29. Notes to this selection appear at the end of the chapter.)

More on the Purpose of Man and the 'World to Come'

The purpose (of existence) is none other than the world to come, and for its sake is all the endeavor. Therefore, this (sage, in the Mishnah) who apprehends the truth looks to the final end (purpose) and has left everything else and said: 'All Israel has a portion in the world to come.' And although this is the purpose, it is not proper for one who wishes to serve (God) from love that he should serve in order to achieve the future world, as we have explained previously, rather he should serve in the way I shall explain; and this is that if he already believes that there is knowledge which has reached the prophets according to which God informed them that the virtues are such-and-such, then he is obligated in that he is upright to draw close to the virtues and avoid the vices, and if he does this he has perfected the human nature[1] and is distinguished from the animals. And since he is made a perfected man, one of the qualities of man which nothing can prevent is that his soul shall live by its intellectual existence, and this is the future world, as we have explained it. This is the meaning of their saying: 'Be not like the horse or the mule which have no understanding' [Psalm 32.9]; that is, the thing which keeps them from being wild is an external thing like the bit and the bridle, but man should not be so, rather what prevents him should be from a faculty of his soul, i.e., his human nature when it is perfect. This keeps him from those things which perfection prevents, which are called vices, and admonishes him about those things by which he is perfected, and they are called virtues. This is what appears to me from all their words in this lofty matter [in which] there is tremendous significance [*al-aẓīm al-*khaṭar; *Kafiḥ understood this as "danger," which is another meaning, but which doesn't seem likely to me]*.

I intend to compose a book in which I shall gather all the allegories found in the Talmud and elsewhere and clarify them and explain them with an explanation fitting the truth, and bring proofs for all this from the words (of the sages), and reveal what of them is literal and what a parable and what occurred in a dream and they mentioned it in plain language as though it occurred in a waking state.[2] In that composition, I shall clarify all the things which I have mentioned in these my words (here) as samples, so that you may compare them...

(Here he begins to explain those exceptions to the statement that all Israel has a share in the world to come, enumerated in the Mishnah:)

Epiquros ("Epicurean") is an Aramaic word[3], the meaning of which is making light and showing contempt for the Torah or sages of the Torah, and therefore this name is applied in general to one who does not believe in the foundations of the Torah or is contemptuous of a scholar or his teacher [*Sanhedrin* 99b].

Extra-canonical books (*one who reads these is said to have no portion in the world to come*), these are the books of the *minin*.[4] And so also the books of Ben Sira, who was a man who composed books of delusions in matters of physiognomy in which there is no wisdom or benefit, but a waste of time in vain things, like these books, found among the Arabs, of chronology and the customs of kings and the geneology of Arabic tribes and books of song,[5] and the likes of these of books in which there is no wisdom and no physical benefit but only a waste of time.

One who utters an incantation for a wound.[6] Specifically by spitting, for there is in this contempt for the Name of God.

One who pronounces the Name (of God) in its letters (the Tetragrammaton)...

They (the sages) already mentioned other things besides these which one who does them has no share in the world to come; they said: 'One who embarrasses *(literally, whitens the face of)* his fellow by words has no portion in the world to come,' and so one who calls his fellow by a nickname (*which is insulting or embarrassing*) [*B.M.* 58 b]. And so one who exalts hmself by the disgrace of his fellow [Jerusalem T. *Ḥagigah* 2.1]. This is because not one of these deeds can come, even if they are light in the opinion of the perpetrator, except from a soul which is lacking, which has not reached perfection, and is not worthy of the life of the world to come.

(Introduction to Commentary on Mishnah *Sanhedrin* 10.1; tr. Kafiḥ, *Neziqin*, pp. 140-41; ed. Rabinowitz, pp. 132-36)

The Future World and a Ball Game

And now I shall begin to speak of what I intended (the future world). Know that just as a blind person cannot apprehend colors, nor one who is deaf sounds, nor the eunuch the delights of sexual intercourse, so bodies cannot apprehend spiritual pleasures. And just as the fish does not recognize the element of fire because he dwells in the opposite (water), so one does not know in this physical world the pleasures of the spiritual world, since we have no other pleasure than the pleasure of the body and the sensations of the senses of eating and drinking and sexual intercourse, and anything outside of this is non-existent for us and we do not recognize it or apprehend it at first glance, but only after great investigation. The thing is so because we are in a physical world and can only apprehend its pleasures, but the spiritual pleasures are eternal without cessation; there is between them and these (physical) pleasures no relation in any manner at all, and it is not proper for us according to the Torah nor according to the godly of the philosophers to say that the angels and the stars and the spheres have no pleasure, for they have a very great pleasure in what they intellect of the Creator by which they are in an eternal state of pleasure without cessation. There is no physical pleasure for them and they do not apprehend it, since they have no senses as we do by which they may apprehend what we apprehend.

But we also, if we are purified and reach that same level after death, shall not (any longer) apprehend physical pleasures nor desire them; no more than a king, majestic in his kingdom, would abandon his kingdom and return to play with a ball with youths in the streets of the city, even though there was a time in the past undoubtedly when he valued playing ball more than the kingdom, in his youth when he did not know the difference between the two things. Thus today we value bodily pleasures over the spiritual. And if you consider these two pleasures, you will find the inferiority of the one and the advantage of the other, even in this world, for we find the majority of people and perhaps all of them placing on their souls and bodies insurmountable labor and effort to achieve greatness or honor, and yet this is not a pleasure of eating or drinking. So, many people value vengeance against their enemies more than many of the physical pleasures, and many avoid the greatest physical pleasure that could be because of their fear that there could result shame or reproach from people, or in order to achieve a good reputation. And if this is our situation in this physical world, how much more in the spiritual world which is the world to come in which our souls shall intellect the Creator, similar to what the upper Causes (the separate intellects) intellect, or more. That pleasure cannot be distinguished or described, and no parable can be found with which to compare it, but what the prophet said, amazed in his bones, 'How great is Your goodness which You have laid up for those who fear You; which You have performed for those who trust in You' [Psalm 31.20].

Thus the sages said 'The world to come has neither eating nor drinking, washing or anointing, or sexual intercourse; but the righteous sit with their crowns on their heads enjoying the radiance of the Divine Presence' [*Berakhot* 17a]. Their intention in saying 'crowns on their heads' is the existence of the soul in its cognized [state] (i.e., the active intellect), and since it (the active intellect) and He are one, as the expert philosophers have mentioned in ways I shall show you here.[1] And they said 'they delight in the radiance of the Divine Presence,' that is, those souls delight in what they intellect of the Creator, as the holy creatures (*of Ezekiel's vision*) and the other degrees of angels (delight) in what they intellect of His existence.

The final end and happiness[2] is to attain this elevated group and to be in this situation and existence of the soul—as we have said—without end, in the existence of the Creator who is the cause of its (the soul's) existence, in apprehending Him, as is explained in the First Philosophy.[3] This is the greatest good, to which no other good or pleasure compares, and how can existence without end be compared to something which is lost? For he said: 'That it may be well with you and that you may prolong your days' [Deuteronomy 22.7], and a tradition came to their (the sages') hands explaining it 'that it may be well with you' in the world which is all prolonged [*Qiddushin* 39b *Ḥullin* 142a; cf. *Guide* III.28].

(Introduction to *Sanhedrin* 10.1, sources as in the previous selection: ed. Kafiḥ, pp. 137-38; ed. Rabinowitz, pp. 123-26; cf. the very faulty translation in Isadore Twersky, ed., *Maimonides Reader* [N.Y., 1972], pp. 410-12.)

Categories of Speech

The sage has said, 'In the multitude of words, sin is not lacking' [Proverbs 10.19], and the meaning of the thing is that the majority of words are superfluous (or) sinful, as I shall now explain; for when a man increases speech he will necessarily sin, since there will certainly be in his speech at least one word which is not proper to be said, and one of the signs of a wise man is paucity of speech, as they have said, 'a fence for wisdom is silence' [*Pirqey Avot* 3.13]. A multiplicity of speech is a sign of fools; 'a fool's voice in a multitude of words' [Eccles. 5.2]. The sages have already said that a paucity of speech is a sign of good breeding[1] and of pure lineage; they said, 'Silence is lineage' [*Qiddushin* 71b].[2]

It says in the Book of Ethics[3] that one of the saints[4] appeared to maintain much silence, so that he did not speak only a very little. They said to him, Why are you so silent? He said, I examined speech and found it divided into four categories. The first category is speech which is entirely damage in which there is no benefit, such as cursing people and profane words and the like, and this speech is complete folly. The second category is speech which consists partly of damage and partly of benefit, as to praise a man in order to gain something from him, but in that praise there is that which angers (the man's) enemy with the result that he harms the one he praises, and therefore one must refrain from this and not speak also in this category of speech. The third category is that in which there is neither benefit nor harm, like the majority of the stories of the people: how the walls of the city were built, how such and such a palace was built, a description of the beauty of a certain house, the praise of the fruits of a certain city, and the like of such things which are only superfluous and have no benefit in them. And the fourth category is that which is entirely beneficial, such as the speech concerning knowledge and ethics, and the speech of man on matters relating to his life and continuous existence, and of these it is worthy to speak. He said, Everytime I hear speech I examine it, and if I find it of this fourth category, I speak about it, and if it is of the rest I am silent. The scholars of ethics said, Consider this man and his wisdom! He withholds from his mouth three-fourths of speech, and this is wisdom according to which it is proper to conduct oneself.

And I say that speech is divided according to the requirement of our Torah into five categories: decreed, prohibited, despised, suitable (desirable), and permitted. The first category is the decreed, which is the reading of the Torah and learning it and studying its commentary, and this is a positive commandment concerning which we were commanded: 'and speak of them' [Deuteronomy 6.7.]; and it is like (similar to) all the commandments,[5] and there has already been written concerning this learning more than this book could contain even a portion.

The second category is the prohibited and cautioned-against, such as false testimony, lying, slander, calumny, and reviling. Many scriptural passages teach about this category, and included in it are obscene speech and gossip.

The third category is despised speech, and this is speech in which there is no benefit to the soul of man, neither a pious deed nor sin;[6] like the majority of the stories of people on what happened and what was, and how a certain king behaves in his palace, and what was the cause of the death of so-and-so or the wealth of so-and-so, and this is called by the sages 'idle talk.' Righteous (ethical) people exert themselves to refrain from this speech. It is said of Rav, the student of R. Ḥiyya, that he never spoke idle talk in all his days.[7] Also of this category is that a man disparages a virtue or praises a vice, whether ethical or rational.

The fourth category is the suitable, and it is the praise of rational and ethical virtues, and the derogation of these two types of vices, and to arouse the soul to this through prose and poetry[8] and to restrain it from (the vices) by the same means. So also the praise of the pious and relating the importance of their virtues in order to enhance their behavior in the eyes of men that they walk in their ways; and to denounce evil men and their vices to cause their deeds and reputations to be despised in the eyes of men that they separate from them and not walk in their ways. This category, that is, learning the good virtues and removal from the base qualities, is called 'the way of the earth' (*in talmudic language; proper conduct*).

The fifth category is the permitted, which is the speech concerning what relates to man in his business and income, his food and drink and clothing, and the rest of his needs. This permitted (speech) is neither suitable nor despised; rather, if he wishes, he may speak as much as he wants about it, and if he wishes, he may be silent. But in this category what should be chosen for man is a minimum of speech, and the books of ethics warn against multiplicity of words about it. But the prohibited and despised (types of speech), it is unnecessary to say or to command, one should be silent in these completely. However, the prescribed and the suitable, if a man were able to speak of these all the days of his life, this would be the desired end, except that he requires with this two things, one that his deeds be fitted to his words, as they say, 'Pleasant are words that go forth from the mouth of those who do them' [*Tosefta, Yevamot*, ch. 8, at end], and on this matter it is said here: 'Not the learning is the essence, but the deed' [*Pirqey Avot* 1.16] and the sages said to the righteous who teaches the lofty virtues, 'Expound, and you are worthy to expound' [*Tosefta, ibid.*; cf. *B.B.* 75a, *Sanhedrin* 100a]. The prophet said, 'Rejoice in the Lord, O you righteous: praise is comely for the upright' [Psalm 33.1]. And the second thing (which is required) is brevity, that he endeavor to increase topics in a few words, and not the opposite; and this is their saying, 'Always let a man teach his student by way of brevity' [*Pesaḥim* 3b].

And know that poems made in any language are not examined except according to their subject, and their manner is as the way of speech, as we have already divided it. And I had to explain this even though it is simple because I have seen elders and pure (men) of our community when they were at a wine banquet, whether it is a wedding or some other place, and were a man to recite an Arabic poem, even if the words of that poem were praise of courage or generosity[9] which is of the category of suitable (desirable), or praise of the wine, they would protest this with every manner of protest and not permit it to be heard; but if the poet were to recite a Hebrew *muwashshaḥ*[10] they would not protest it even though its speech (subject) is of the prohibited or despised category. And this is complete folly, since speech is not prohibited or permitted, suitable, despised, and decreed to one who utters it because of the language in which it is said, but because of the subject. For if the subject of a poem were purity (or virtue), it would be required to recite it in whatever language, but if its subject were vice, it would be required to refrain from it in whatever language. But in my opinion one shoud add that if there were two *muwashshaḥāt* with the intent both of them to arouse the power to vice (lust) and praise it and draw the soul to it, which is a vice, and this is of the category of the despised because it stimulates and arouses a base quality, and one of the poems were in Hebrew and the other Arabic or the vernacular,[11] listening to the Hebrew one and speaking it would be more despised according to the opinion of the Torah because of the sanctity of the language, since it is not desirable to utilize it except for lofty matters; and all the more so if is added to this (in the poem) the use of a passage of the Torah or Song of Songs on that subject, in which case it departs from the despised category and becomes of the category of prohibited and cautioned against, for the Torah prohibits making prophetic language types of song of depravity and vileness.[12]

Inasmuch as we have mentioned gossip in the category of prohibited speech, I shall explain it, and mention of it some of the words of the sages, since men are in great darkness about this, and it is the greatest sin which man sins against man constantly; especially in that the sages said that 'particles (small amounts) of gossip, a man is not saved from every day' [*B.B.* 164b], and would that it not be actual gossip itself. Gossip is the telling of the vices of men and their faults and the debasing of a Jew in whatever manner, and even if he is debased as is said, for gossip is not that one should lie about a person and ascribe to him what he did not do—which is called giving forth a bad name on one's fellow—but gossip is disparagement of a man and even of actions which he definitely has done, and one who says it sins and the one who hears it sins; (as) they said, 'Three are killed by gossip, the one who says it, the one who hears it, and the one of whom it is said' [*ᶜArkhin* 15b]. And they said, 'One who receives it more than one who says it' [See *Shabbat* 56b]. 'Particles of gossip' are hints to the defects of a person without saying them explicitly. Solomon said of one who hints and indicates that he does not know what is understood from his words and that he did not intend that but intended another matter: 'As a madman who throws firebrands, arrows, and death, so is a man who tricks his neighbor, and says: But I was only joking!' [Proverbs 26. 18-19]. Once one of the sages praised the writing of a certain scribe, which was shown to him at a large banquet, and the rabbi rebuked the one who praised the writing and said 'Desist from gossip' [*B.B.* 164b]; that is to say, in that which you praise him in public you cause him contempt, for he has his friends and he has his enemies, and his enemy when he hears his praise will have to relate his faults...

(Commentary on *Pirqey Avot* 1.16, ed. Kafiḥ, op. cit., pp. 272-74; Arabic text ed. with Hebrew tr., E. Baneth in *Jubelscrhift zum siebzigsten Geburtstag des Dr. Israel Hildesheimer* [Berlin, 1890], pp. 69-75; inaccurate English translation in Twersky, *Maimonides Reader*, pp. 390-93)

Letter to Ḥasdai ha-Levy

(This important letter was written in response to questions addressed to Maimonides by Ḥasdai ha-Levy ha-Sefardy [''of Spain''] in Alexandria,[1] and the reply was given to one of Maimonides' students to transcribe, but not in the exact language of Maimonides; thus, it is a paraphrase in Hebrew):

Know that the philosophical sages did not decide to establish one of their words except by a clear proof, such that there is no rebuttal for it. The first groups (of philosophers) who were before Plato denied God, and brought proofs that the world is eternal and there is no mover for the sphere(s). The later groups admitted (the existence of) God and that the world was created, like the opinion of our master Moses. Other of the later groups admitted (the existence of) God but said that the world is eternal and that God has no purpose of creating, but the world is his resulting effect[2] and He is the cause, as the candle is the cause of its light and a pole the cause of its shadow. And it is impossible for a cause to precede its caused effect, nor for a caused effect (to be) without a cause. Of these three disagreements no clear proof was established for any of them; only inconsequential proofs were brought by each of them for his words, but no clear proof. But there is clear to me from their words a clear proof for God, for in the end, even the eternalists[3] agree that there is a cause above the sphere, for it has matter and form; and there is no third way, either eternal or created, and both of them are impossible without something above them. Thus you must say (it is) possibly eternal, possibly created; and if so, there is certainly found there a God. To say that the world is neither eternal nor created is a thing which is not possible. But on the act of creation, there has not been clarified for me a clear proof and the thing is ambiguous, and there is no power to disprove one of (the opinions: created or eternal) from a clear proof. And I say that the knowledge of man is finite, and all the time the soul is in the body it is not able to know what is above nature (supernatural causes); since it resides in nature, it is impossible for it to look and see what is above. Therefore, when knowledge goes to observe above, it cannot, for the thing is higher than it; but everything which is in nature it is able to know and to observe.

And the sages of Israel, even though Ben Azai said: 'All the sages of Israel in my eyes are like the skin of garlic' [*Bikkurim* 58a], he was not able to observe.[4] This is proof that no clear proof stands for any of the three opinions—and certainly there is no other (opinion). Know that there is there a level of knowledge higher than that of the philosophers, and it is prophecy, and prophecy is another world in which proof and discussion do not apply, for since it is made clear that this is prophecy there remains no place for proof. So you see that they did not request of a prophet proof except on the prophecy itself, whether it is prophecy or not, and this is called 'miracle,' but they did not request a proof above the prophecy; for it is above proof, and not proof above it. Proof is the beginning of knowledge, that is, clear proof; therefore, if it stands the test of knowledge, it convinces. And the prophet is he who is able to arrive at what is above nature, and Moses our teacher was the end of prophecy and there is nothing in prophecy above him.

And since the thing is so, how is it possible to establish a proof on words of prophecy, when prophecy is above proof and proof does not reach to the place where prophecy does? Therefore, it is impossible for proof to stand in the place where prophecy stands. It results in your saying that a man does not contest a thing unless he denies the prophecy of Moses our teacher and says he was not a prophet, but if he admits that he was a prophet, he will not continue to ask for proof; and this is the principle of the true faith upon which we depend, that Moses our teacher was a prophet of the Lord and his words are prophecy and above proof. But to argue from the way of wisdom which is beneath prophecy, nothing will come out clearly, for it is not possible to arrive at it. To what is this to be likened?—to one who thought to collect all the water of the world in one little jug.

Natural Religion

And that which you said that a man could claim that the division of religions is from nature, this is true according to the laws[5] which are laws of the opinions of the body,[6] but man cannot contest (this by) the laws of the soul, since the soul is not of nature and not the result[7] of the sphere; but the customs and opinions of the body change with nature, and the wisdom of the soul does not change with nature and is not dependent on it. Therefore, scholars of medicine said that the opinions of the soul are according to the foundation of the body (physical constitution), until one scholar came who learned and received (knowledge) aside from whom he read, and became wise, and said that his soul admonished the opinions to (conform) to its opinion and it (the soul) has dominion over nature. And so the sages of truth, our rabbis upon whom be peace, said that 'All is in the hands of heaven except for the fear of heaven' [*Berakhot* 33b]. And so of Cain it says: 'To you shall be [sin's] desire, yet you may rule over it' [Genesis 4.7].

Movement of the Spheres and Prophecy of Moses

And that which you asked about the reason for the sphere, the majority of sages agreed that it is impossible for it to turn without a Turner, just as it is impossible for there to be an action or something acted upon without an actor. And if this (the agent for the motion of the spheres) were in nature, there would be an end to its circuit (the motion of the sphere), since nature has an end and limit to its power. But since the sphere moves eternally without stopping, and there is no end to its circuit, it is known that its power is from God, and no man disagrees with this except one who denies God. The spheres themselves have souls and opinions and recognize and know the Rock of the worlds (God) and of their wisdom and opinions.[8]

And the speech which was joined with Moses our teacher certainly was a created voice found in nature. But many said that there was (in him) no physical speech and no voice, but that his soul was grasping the opinions of the upper intelligences and understanding and hearing in the way of true speech, which is the logic of divine opinions which we are not able to understand how it is.[9] And if scripture did not teach saying: 'and he heard the voice speaking to him' [Numbers 7.89], I would agree with this (above opinion); furthermore, the passage about the second tablets [Exodus 34.1ff.; but probably the reference is to Exodus 33.17ff.] does not go (according to) this. Therefore, we may only say that it was a created (physical) voice...

Righteous Gentiles

And what you asked about the nations, know that the Merciful One demands the heart,[10] and things (follow) after the heart. Therefore the sages of truth, our rabbis upon whom be peace, said, 'The righteous of the nations of the world have a share in the world to come,'[11] if they apprehend what is desirable to apprehend of the knowledge of the Creator and improve their souls by good virtues. And there is no doubt that everyone who improves his soul by the fitness of virtues and fitness of wisdom through belief in the Creator certainly is of the children of the world to come. Therefore the sages of truth, our rabbis upon whom be peace, said, 'Even a gentile who occupies himself with the Torah of Moses is like a high priest.'[12] The whole essence of the thing is that the purpose of the Torah of Moses is the improvement of the soul for the Creator, as David said: 'I have set the Lord always before me; surely He is at my right hand, I shall not be moved' [Psalm 16.8]; nor was Moses praised except in this: 'Now the man Moses was very humble...,'[Numbers 12.3], and that is the end of fitness of the soul. And so the sages of truth, our rabbis, said, 'Be exceedingly humble...,' [*Pirqey Avot* 4.4]. There happened that a sage, a great philosopher, traveled in a ship and sat in the place of trash and one of the sailors came and urinated on that place, and (the philosopher) raised his head and laughed. They asked him, Why do you laugh? He replied, Because now it is made clear to me with certainty that my soul is on a high level, for it did not at all feel the humiliation of this thing. And so the sages said, 'Just as wisdom made a crown for its head, humility made a heel for its sandal' [Jer. *Shabbat* 1.3, with a slight change] because it is the end of good qualities.

The philosophers said that is is remote to find a man perfect and complete in virtues and wisdom, and if he is found he is called 'man of God,' and certainly such a one is of the highest level. And this is the will (purpose) of the Torah and the wisdom of the commandments, to improve the soul by its virtues and by belief in the Creator. Therefore scripture says: 'Surely this great nation is a wise and understanding people' [Deut. 4.6]. And there is no doubt in this that the patriachs and Noah and Adam, who did not at all observe the words of the Torah, are not sons of Gehenna (Hell); rather, certainly since they attained and apprehended what is desirable to be improved, they are of the upper level. Nor is this thing, in truth, dependent upon fasts and prayer and lamentation without knowledge and faith, because in this God is near in their mouths and far from their hearts. The essence of everything is that there is no thing which stands for ever and eternally except the Creator.

(Moses b. Maimon, **Qoveṣ teshuvot**, ed. Aaron Lichtenberg [Leipzig, 1859; photo rpt. Farnborough, England, 1969] II, 23a-24a. The translation here is not of the complete text of the letter.)

Notes

The Purpose of Man

[1] The importance of carefully consulting the Arabic text is seen in comparing Judah al-Ḥarizi's medieval Hebrew translation here, where he used the strange Hebrew term *koḥo ha-peniniyah*, which appears almost unintelligible. In his edition (Moses b. Maimon, **Haqdamot le-feirush ha-mishnah** [Jerusalem, 1961, p. 76, n. 2]), Mordecai Rabinowitz provided a learned note trying to explain the term on the basis of texts of Solomon Ibn Gabirol (*Improvement of the Moral Qualities*, ed. [Arabic] and tr. Stephen S. Wise [N.Y., 1901], p. 1, line 9 of text, p. 29 and n. 4 of tr.; the medieval Hebrew translation as *Goren nakhon, tiqqun middot ha-nefesh* [Luneville, 1807; photo rpt. Jerusalem, 1967], p. 1; "*Keter malkhut*" poem in Ibn Gabirol, *Selected Religious Poems*, ed. Israel Davidson and tr. Israel Zangwill [Philadelphia, 1923], p. 101, line 297. Rabinowitz supplied no specific references), where the term apparently means "shimmering, luminous," and thus perhaps "illuminating power, or faculty" may be what the Hebrew translator intended. Nevertheless, the Arabic term used by Maimonides here, and incidentally the same term is used by Ibn Gabirol, is simply *jūhar*, which means "essence." The cause of al-Ḥarizi's confusion is difficult to explain. Rosner has used only that Hebrew translation, and so renders it as "internal strength," with a very improbable explanation in his footnote (p. 123 and n. 678). Ibn Gabirol's work was undoubtedly known to Maimonides, and may have influenced him.

[2] Not only is this the opposite of the classical *mens sana in corpore sano* ("sound mind in a sound body") notion, it is an apparent rejection of Plato (cf. Averroes' *Commentary on Plato's Republic*, ed. and tr. E. I. J. Rosenthal [Cambridge, 1969] pp. 123-24, and the corrected translation by Ralph Lerner, *Averroes on Plato's Republic* [Ithaca, N.Y., 1974], p. 17, and Plato, *Republic* 376 E). See in general Aristotle, *Nic. Ethics*

VII.14; Moses b. Maimon, **Guide**, pp. 433-34, 503, etc. (tr. Pines).

[3] *Nic Ethics* X.7.1177 a 15; cf. *Politics* VII.1.10.

[4] I have so far not succeeded in finding the source for this.

[5] The world was divided into seven climatic zones according to Greek and medieval notions, and the first and seventh were considered generally uninhabitable.

Maimonides expresses here views on the existence of the majority of people in order to serve the needs of the scholar-philosopher which are, of course, akin to those of Plato and Aristotle in classical philosophy, and al-Fārābī and Ibn Bājja in Muslim philosophy. It is interesting that here he appears to ridicule the merchant, when his own brother David was just such a merchant and died in a storm at sea not long before this was written.

More on the Purpose of Man

[1] Not that he has reached a state of complete perfection, but that he has fulfilled the conditions necessary for being a human and not an animal.

[2] This probably refers to the book which he called "Book of Correspondence" (Comparison) which, along with the "Book of Prophecy," he stated his intention to compose (in Introduction to the Commentary on the Mishnah). In his introduction to **Guide** (p.9 of Pines' tr.), he explains why he decided after all not to compose these books (cf. also the statement of his son Abraham on this in his treatise on these subjects, in Moses b. Maimon, **Qoveṣ teshuvot**, ed. Lichtenberg [Leipzig, 1859, photo rpt. 1969] II, 40. The word *derashot* does not mean the same as Midrashim, as Pines there (p. 9) says, and Maimonides already discussed this in the Introduction to the Commentary on the Mishnah, and so also his son Abraham in the place cited.

[3] It is not, of course; rather Greek. In the Talmud and elsewhere, the term strangely came to mean not a hedonist, but a heretic of the worst kind. Probably Maimonides means here that

the term is used in Aramaic texts, and not that it is Aramaic in origin.

[4] On the subject of "extra-canonical books," see especially Saul Lieberman, *Hellenism in Jewish Palestine* (N.Y., 1950), pp. 108-09 and the sources cited in the notes (the explanation that Ben Sira was prohibited because of confusion with a biblical book, cited there in the name of David Frankel, is improbable; indeed, the reason for the objection is not clear to us at all, and is even more puzzling in Maimonides since it is clear from citations that Jewish writers of Spain had the actual text of Ben Sira). *Minim* is a problematic term, often meaning simply "heretics," but sometimes "Christians."

[5] Note that he does *not* say here "poetry," as has often (erroneously) been thought. The Arabic is *kutub al-aghānī*, "books of song;" however, the objection to these is again difficult to understand, for such compositions were not mere books of melodies, but serious philosohical and logical treatises which should therefore be considered among the prerequisites for the study of metaphysics (cf. **Guide** I. 34). On the other hand, Baḥya Ibn Paquda, whose influence on Maimonides was far grater than has yet been realized, although he specifically included music among the "wisdoms" or sciences, made it clear that he had little use for collections of poetry, stories, parables and proverbs (*Ḥovot ha-levavot*, ed. A. Ẓifroniy [Tel Aviv, 1964], introduction, p. 6, and "Gate 5," p. 364). It is probably this kind of work which Maimonides intended; namely, collections of stories, parables, proverbs and also poetry which often used this general title. (Both Kafiḥ and Rabinowitz erred in their notes on this in associating it with Maimonides' dislike of poetry, which is another matter altogether.)

[6] It is interesting (and ironic, considering the previous prohibition against the book) to compare what Ben Sira says about the doctor who heals the wound by the aid of God (Ben Sira 38.1-4, see the translation in *The Apocrypha and Pseudepigrapha of the Old Testament*, tr. R. H. Charles [Oxford, 1913] I, 449 and the notes there citing parallel sources—to which add *B.Q.* 85a and *Berakhot* 60a).

The Future World and a Ball Game

[1] This is a highly technical and important philosophical passage, for which I had recourse to the original Arabic text. For this expression, "He and it are one," see the commentary on Song of Songs by Maimonides' contemporary (*not*, as often said, his student) Joseph Ibn ᶜAqnin, *Hitgallut ha-sodot ve-hofaᶜat ha-meorot*, ed. (Judeo-Arabic) and tr. (Hebrew) A.S. Halkin (Jerusalem, 1964), p. 89, line 18 and p. 403, line 8, and cf. Moses b. Naḥman, *Kitvey ha-Ramban*, ed. Chavel, II, 307; Azriel of Gerona, *Peirush ha-aggadah*, p. 20, lines 5-6; the *dīwān* of al-Hallaj ed. Massignon in *Journal Asiatique* (1931), Nos. 41, 47, 57. Thus, this expression has a long, almost mystical, tradition.

[2] On this, see my "Attaining 'Happiness' (*Eudaimonia*) in Medieval Muslim and Jewish Philosophy," *Centerpoint* 4 (1981): 21-32. (On a recent television show, Mortimer Adler and a professor of philosophy discussed the concept of "happiness" in Aristotle in a manner which indicated that neither had any real notion of what Aristotle said on the subject.)

[3] Not actually the *Metaphysics*, but *Nic. Ethics* X.117a 11ff., 1178b 7-23, 1179a 17-32; cf. *Eudemian Ethics* VII.15 1249b 13-16.

Categories of Speech

[1] See the explanation of this term in Kafiḥ's edition, p. 272, n. 79.

[2] Cf. **Mishneh Torah,** *Madaᶜ, "Deᶜot"* 2. 4-5.

[3] Not Aristotle, but apparently one of the many works in Arabic on ethics, etc. (cf. Kafiḥ, *op. cit.*, n. 81). The same story is told by Solomon Ibn Gabirol, *Mivḥar ha-peninim*, "*Shaᶜar ha-shetiqah*" at the end.

[4] See Kafiḥ, *op. cit.*, n. 82 on this word. I believe the translation "saint" is closer to the Arabic meaning than "sage." Baneth translated it "*nazir*."

[5] See Kafiḥ, *op. cit.*, p. 273, n. 87. I don't understand the

problem here, for the Arabic text reads exactly as I have translated it, and it does not appear that it can refer to the well-known idea that "study of Torah is equal to all the commandments," but rather that this is (actually) one of the commandments.

[6] These are well-known terms in Muslim theology and law, *ma^{c}ṣiya* and *ṭā^{c}a*; therefore, I don't understand Kafiḥ's translation here. Baneth translated the first word as *ṣedaqah*, "charity," when *ṣedeq*, "righteousness," might have been better.

[7] The source is confused; cf. Kafiḥ, *op. cit.*, p. 373, n. 89.

[8] *Al-khuṭāb wa'l-ash^{c}ār*. Sometimes, the first word means "orations," as in a mosque, but the combination of words usually means "prose and poetry." Here is an overlooked place where Maimonides, far from opposing poetry, urges its use (he no doubt meant religious or ethical works, of course).

[9] Kafiḥ's translation, p. 374, line 2, is not correct and the original medieval Hebrew translation is right.

[10] This is a rhymed strophic poem in which the last couplet is in Arabic or Romance. Maimonides deliberately and intentionally used this term, and not just "poem" (as all the translations render it), because such poems particularly were devoted to the topics he mentions.

[11] *Aghamī* does not mean "Persian," as Kafiḥ, p. 374, n. 98, says, but "vernacular;" here, specifically Romance is meant.

[12] Kafiḥ's translation is not nearly strong enough here.

Letter to Ḥasdai ha-Levy

[1] I have been unable to find any information on him other than in Heimann (Ḥayyim) Michael, *Or ha-ḥayyim* (Frankfurt a. M., 1891), p. 420. I would be grateful if anyone else has further information.

[2] cf. **Guide** I. 69; especially p. 166 of Pines' translation, "that which is caused," which is rendered by Ibn Tibbon by the same term, *^{c}alul*, as is used here.

[3] *Ma^{c}etiqim*, from *^{c}atiq*; a unique term (?); often the word was used to mean "translators," under the influence of Arabic *naqal* (cf. Mosheh Goshen-Gottstein, *Taḥbirah ve-millonah shel ha-lashon ha-^{c}ivrit she-be-teḥum hashpa^{c}atah shel ha-^{c}aravit* [Jerusalem, 1951], p. 227). This meaning is not noted in Hebrew dictionaries at all.

[4] The text may be a little confused here. Possibly Maimonides intended that even Ben Azai, in spite of being superior to the other sages, could not observe what is above (cf. the well-known story [*Ḥagigah* 14b] of the four men who went into paradise; Ben Azai gazed and died).

[5] *Nimusim* (Gr. *nomos*), a term difficult to render in English, it basically means governing principles and sometimes specifically promulgated law.

[6] Probably he is referring here to political science, or the "welfare of the body." Cf. the basic discussion of this in **Guide** III.27, and especially the chapter on political science, *ibid*. II. 40, where he also discusses *nomos* (pp. 382-84 of Pines' translation).

[7] *^{c}Alul*; cf. note 2 above. The soul is not "of nature" because it is from God.

[8] That the spheres are the separate intellects, and all that is involved with this, is discussed at length in **Guide** II. 3-5.

[9] I have not been able to find the source for "many said" either in the Talmud or in any of of the midrashim which I checked. On Moses in general in relation to what is said here, see **Guide** I. 54.

[10] Although this has become a proverbial statement, and is always quoted in the Aramaic version which appears here (*Raḥmana liba ba^{c}iy*), the actual source is Hebrew: "The Holy One, blessed be he" (*Sanhedrin* 106 b).

[11] Again, this is an oft-quoted statement, but it has no actual rabbinic source. The closest is a debate which occurs in *Tosefta Sanhedrin* 13 (ed. Zuckermandel, p. 434), repeated in *Midrash*

Tehillim, ed. Buber (Vilna, 1891), p. 90 (on Ps. 9, section 15, and see Buber's notes there), and cf. also *Sanhedrin* 105a. (The popularity of these expressions in later generations indicates the influence of this letter of Maimonides.

[12] *Sifra* 86b; cf. *Sanhedrin* 59a.

Knowledge of God and God's Knowledge: Two Epistemological Problems in Maimonides

(20th International Congress on Medieval Studies, Kalamazoo, Michigan, May 9, 1985)

The subject of knowledge in the thought of Maimonides is unquestionably one of the most important and fundamental topics with which he dealt, yet it is astonishing to realize that there has so far been no systematic discussion of this in any of the scholarly literature.[1]

The focus of this paper is not on the broader subject of knowledge in general in Maimonides' philosophy, but rather on the more limited related notions of the knowledge of, or about, God and God's knowledge. By the latter, furthermore, we do not mean knowledge as an attribute of God, which has in fact been discussed quite thoroughly by Wolfson and others[2], but the question of how God may be said to "know" anything.

The importance of these notions, and their correlation, may be seen in the fact that when Maimonides composed the only work which he wrote in Hebrew, the **Mishneh Torah**, often called the "Code of Jewish Law," written in Hebrew precisely so that all people in whatever land could read and understand it easily, he made the first book in the first volume of that code the "book of knowledge." Franz Rosenthal has demonstrated that in this he was following a ususal practice of Muslim jurisprudence, but the important point for our consideration is that in such a work, written for the masses and not for philosophers, Maimonides considered it essential to set forth as requirements of Jewish law the possession of certain knowledge.[3] Here he states, chapter 2, law 10 of the first treatise ("Foundations of the Torah"):

> The Holy One, blessed be he, recognizes his true [essence] and knows it as it is, and he does not know with a knowing which is external to him, as we know [something]; for we and our knowledge are not

> one...You must say that he is the knower, and he is the known, and he is the knowing itself all in one...

This is my translation, for as I said in another recent paper on Maimonides (and this provoked some laughter; sympathetic, but laughter nonetheless), none of the English translations of this book is accurate. Well, it is a fact, and the carelessness of translators of Hebrew works is proverbial, but it is particularly deplorable here, for if this passage is not translated exactly as Maimonides wrote it, the entire point is missed. The point is that this is a profound philosophic concept, with roots in Aristotle and Plotinus and similarities also in Muslim writers, as I have demonstrated elsewhere.[4]

Now, in **Guide of the Perplexed**, his philosophical *magnum opus*, Maimonides again refers to this as a "generally admitted" saying of the philosophers: "that He is the intellect as well as the intellectually cognizing subject [the Arabic here is *ᶜāqil*, therefore "process of intellecting" would be a better translation] and the intellectually cognized object." There he says that he has already mentioned this in the great compilation, i.e., **Mishneh Torah**.[5] This statement alone should have sufficed to send scholars scurrying in search of the sources he utilized, but they have not done so. Even Pines was content with a vague reference to Aristotle's *Metaphysics*.[6]

Obviously, Maimonides considered it essential for the average Jew, not just the philosophically trained, to understand this conception of God. Equally important in his view was the understanding of the nature of knowledge about God. Thus, he concluded his "Code" with the book called "Judges" in which there appears at the end a discussion of the messianic era, in which, he says, there will be neither famine nor war, jealousy nor strife, and great good will be in abundance. "And the occupation of the entire world will not be other than to know God alone." In the uncensored text, which appears only in the Rome, 1490 and the Constantinople, 1509 editions, at the end of ch. 11, he states: "But the thoughts of the creator of the world are not in the power of man to grasp; for our ways are not his ways, neither are our thoughts his thoughts" (this he says in relation to his discussion of the falseness of Jesus and Muḥammad, whose religions nevertheless have prepared the world for the coming of the true messiah).[7] Even here, though the statement stands on its own simple meaning, it would be possible to apply the philosophical explanation that man cannot grasp the thoughts of God inasmuch as it has already been demonstrated that the knowledge of God is his essence.

There is yet one other important book in which Maimonides discusses this subject in a manner which, as we shall see, is very relevant to the discussion in the **Guide**. This is in his **Eight Chapters on Ethics**, which he wrote as an introduction to his commentary on the treatise *Pirqey Avot* ("Ethics of the Fathers") in the *Mishnah*. Here, at the end of the book, he states that it is a maxim of metaphysics that God "does not know by means of knowledge, and does not live by means of life, so that He and His knowledge may be considered two different things in the sense that this is true of man; for man is distinct from knowledge, and knowledge from man, in consequence of which they are two different things." He continues that another maxim is that human reason cannot fully conceive the true essence of God, and that this inability may be compared to the inability to gaze at the sun; not because of the weakness of the sun's light, but because of the weakness of the eyes to receive the light. This very same metaphor is used, incidentally, in **Guide** I.59.[8] Finally he concludes there:

> From what we have said, it has been demonstrated also that we cannot comprehend God's knowledge, that our minds cannot grasp it all, for He is His knowledge, and His knowledge is He...All that we can comprehend is that just as we know that God exists so are we congnizant of the fact that He knows. If we are asked, 'What is the nature of God's knowledge?' we answer that we do not know any more than we know the nature of His true existence.[9]

We can see the influence of this passage, written when he was quite young (the commentary on the *Mishnah* generally was completed when he was in his early twenties), on the **Guide** in at least two places. In I.68, in the section already cited, he uses exactly the same analogy of God's life and essence and knowledge and essence which he used in **Eight Chapters** (but which I have not here quoted), that for this reason God and his life are one (the Hebrew expression is *Ḥay Adonai*, "As the Lord lives," or "by the living Lord," not, as Pines translates, "by the Lord the living;" it is a quotation from Ruth 3.13, which Pines apparently didn't recognize). "For his life is not something other than his essence," or as he states in **Eight Chapters**, "the purpose is to denote that God and His life are one."

The second place in the **Guide** where the similarity to what has been said in **Eight Chapters** is most striking is at III.20, where he argues against those philosophers who, while admitting that we are incapable of understanding the true essence of God, think they can apprehend his true knowledge.[10] Maimonides says, on the contrary, "between our knowledge and His knowledge there is nothing in common [he uses here the Arabic term *ishtirāk*, meaning "sharing, association," but in a grammatical, or logical, sense and not the more common theological sense of "association" or polytheism] as there is nothing in common between our essence and His essence." It is only the equivocality, or amphibolous nature, of the term "knowledge" which causes the confusion, "for there is a community [Arabic *mushāraka*] only in the terms, whereas in the true reality of the things there is a difference."[11]

One of the ways in which God's knowledge differs from man's is with regard to knowledge of contingents: God's knowledge of the existence of a thing potentially (*in potentia*) does not in any way require that it come into being actually. In the following chapter he adds to this that man's knowledge is derived from apprehending things, and does not grasp either the future or the infinite, whereas God's knowledge, on the contrary, is the cause of things coming into being. "For through knowing the true reality of His immutable essence, He also knows the totality of what necessarily derives from all His acts."

But is it really definite that man's knowledge is totally different from God's knowledge, and that man cannot comprehend God's knowledge at all? It does not appear that this was Maimonides' own view, for he explains that man, too, before he intellectually cognizes a thing is potentially the "intellectually cognizing subject" (to stick with Pines' translation; perhaps better, he is potentially in the process of intellecting), and when he has actually cognized something, which is to separate the form from the matter, then he is at the level of intellect *in actu (faᶜal al-ᶜaql)*. "For intellect is nothing but the thing [I would translate *maᶜānī* here as "concept"] that is intellectually cognized," by which he means that it is the form which is identical with the intellect.[13] "Whenever, therefore, you assume that an intellect exists *in actu*, that intellect is identical with the apprehension of what has been intellectually cognized." Finally, he concludes this very important discussion there:

> It is accordingly also clear that the numerical unity of the intellect, the intellectually cognizing subject, and the intellectually cognized object does not hold good with reference to the Creator only, but also with reference to every intellect. Thus, in us too, the intellectually cognizing subject, the intellect, and the intellectually cognized object are one and the same thing.

but, only when the human intellect is *in actu*—in the process of intellecting. For, unlike God, we pass from potentiality to actuality only from time to time. Indeed, were it not that man's intellect, or at least his intellecting process, were at least at times the same as God's, it would be totally impossible to know God at all.

This becomes clearer when we consider the fact that there is another peculiar law in the previously mentioned "Book of Knowledge" of the **Mishneh Torah**. This again, has been totally incorrectly translated in all versions. Correctly translated, it states:

> The foundation of all foundations and the pillar of all learning is to know that there is there a First Existent and He is the cause of all existing things; and all the existents in the heavens and the earth and what is between them do not exist except through the essence of his bringing them into existence.[14]

Now this appears in the opening section of the book, which Maimonides titled "Foundations of the Torah." In other words, these are principles which he considers it absolutely essential for every Jew to know and understand. In fact, only a person with a fairly good understanding of Aristotle could make any sense out of this passage at all. I have discussed the implications of all this elsewhere; what is important for us here is to realize that Maimonides considers it not just a philosohical necessity but a practical religious obligation to know God. How is this knowledge to be attained? The answer, in part, is given in **Guide** I.34, where he says that there is no other way to apprehend God than through knowledge of the things which he has made. "It is therefore indispensable to consider all beings as they really are" so that we may obtain true and certain premises about them. He means here not only all the things of nature, but also specifically mentions mathematics, geometry and astronomy.[15] Thus we see that it is only through diligent and comprehensive study of the sciences that knowledge of God is possible.

Maimonides indeed outlines in this chapter, in brief, the necessary prerequisites which must be mastered in order to achieve perfection in the knowledge of God: logic, the mathematical sciences in their proper order, the natural sciences, and then the "divine sciences" (which means philosophy, and specifically metaphysics). Nevertheless, he recognizes that many never fully prepare themselves in one or more of these, and for them he says there is the possibility of acquiring correct opinions from traditional authority; in other words, they are told by others, and even by means of parables, what to believe. If this were not so, it "would lead to all people [so Pines translates, but this is wrong; Arabic *al-nās kāffa* means "the masses," not "all people," which would be absurd!] dying without having known whether there is a deity for the world or whether there is not."[16] Incidentally, and apparently this fact has escaped the notice of the commentators, this is related in a striking manner to what Maimonides says at the end of **Eight Chapters**, that there are those who fail to grasp the notion that God and his knowledge are one to their dying day.[17] This coincides with his general position that the Torah, like all law, aims at two things: welfare of the body (correct actions) and welfare of the soul (correct opinions and beliefs), and the masses are generally taught these things by the Torah through parables and illustrations.

"As for the few solitary individuals," he continues, who achieve perfection, "which constitutes the end to be aimed at, [it] is realized for them only after the above-mentioned preliminary studies." Unlike the masses, the properly trained and prepared (and he enumerates five causes which hinder this preparation) achieve the true knowledge of correct actions through study of political science (as understood by Aristotle and Muslim philosophers such as al-Fārābī) and correct opinions through study of the other sciences and philosophy. Concerning political science, he cites Isaiah 3.3 that such a one is called "wise in crafts" (*ḥakam ḥarashim*), and mentions the pun of the Talmud "When he speaks, all become deaf" (*ḥershim*). Then he adds:

> Consider how, by means of a text of a book [better would be: by the stipulation of the text of scripture] they laid down as conditions of the perfection of the individual his being perfect in the varieties of political regimes as well as in the speculative science.[19]

Maimonides points out that "there is an immense difference between guidance leading to a knowledge of the existence of a thing and an investigation of the true reality of the essence and substance of that thing." Since scripture, which is directed only to the inculcation of generally correct opinions and actions, speaks in parables, the masses have become confused in their knowledge of God, believing literally not only in the attributes ascribed to God—such as knowledge, power, and the like—but even in the corporeality of God. Since they cannot comprehend the existence of anything other than in a physical form and body, so they imagine God to have a body.[20] Maimonides is absolutely opposed to any such notion, of course, and has already stated that there can be no true belief in the unity of God combined with any kind of belief in the corporeality of God, for a body is necessarily twofold, composed of matter and form, and cannot be one.[21] Similarly, people assume that angels have bodies, and

Maimonides says this is because "it is very difficult for man to apprehend, except after strenuous training, that which is pure matter and absolutely devoid of corporeality." Maimonides maintains the position, advocated by Ibn. Sīnā and al-Rāzī, that angels are the separate intellects.[22]

Now it is precisely to escape such erroneous misconceptions, which are not merely mistaken but which in fact prevent man from fulfilling his role and achieving the state of perfection which is required, that the preparation for the acquisition of proper knowledge which he has mentioned is required. This leads us to the question of what is the purpose of knowledge for man.

In his introduction to the commentary on the *Mishnah Zera*ᶜ*im* (sometimes referred to as the general introduction to the Mishnah, *Haqdamah la-mishnah*), Maimonides says we must investigate what is the purpose and end of man. After considering all the activities of man it is found that all of them are only

> to insure his survival in order that there may be perfected in him that unique activity which is the apprehension of the intelligibles and the knowledge of truth [Arabic *ḥaqā'iq*, reality, true nature of things] according to his ability. For it is not possible that the end of man should be to eat and drink or engage in intercourse or build a house or be a king, for all these are accidents which happen to him [i.e., are external to him] and do not add to his essential nature. And further, all these activities are common to him and to the rest of living creatures; but it is the intellect which adds to his essential nature and advances him from a low level to an elevated one, because he has become a man in actuality; for man before he knows something is only like an animal since man is not differentiated from other living creatures except by logic [Arabic *nuṭq*], since he is a logical animal. I mean by 'logic' the apprehension of intelligibles, and the greatest of these is the apprehension of the unity of God, may he be exalted and praised, and all that is connected to it in metaphysical knowledge; for all the rest of knowledge is only a preparation to attain that [metaphysical] knowledge.[23]

It is instructive to compare with this his similar statement in **Guide** I.51: "For being a rational animal [so Pines translates; actually "logical," for Maimonides uses the exact Arabic word which he used in the introduction to the *Mishnah*] is the essence and true reality of man."

Also when discussing the concept of man as microcosm, he says that this notion applies only to man "because of that which is a proprium [special characteristic] of man only, namely, the rational faculty—I mean the intellect, which is the hylic [material or acquired] intellect; something that is not to be found in any of the species of living beings other than man." This in turn recalls the important passage where he first refers to this, at the end of **Guide** I.1: "Now man possesses as his proprium something in him that is very strange as it is not found in anything else that exists in the sublunar sphere, namely intellectual apprehension."[24] Furthermore, this apprehension—which, Shem Tov Ibn Shem Tov correctly observes in his commentary to the **Guide** is the acquired intellect—is like the apprehension of God which also does not require an instrument (i.e., an intermediary sense).[25] Thus, the ultimate perfection of man consists in attaining a level of apprehension which is not unlike that of God, from the point of view of function if not, certainly, of content.

When a man neglects, or does not understand to begin with, that this *is* the ultimate perfection, he confuses other ends as the final end of man. This is what happened with Job, who made his complaints "as long as he had no true knowledge and knew the deity only because of his acceptance of authority, just as the multitude adhering to a law know it." When he lacked certain knowledge (this is a technical concept in Muslim philosophy) he imagined that those things thought to bring happiness, such as health, wealth, and children, are the ultimate goal of man.[26]

Not only does matter interfere with the true apprehension of God when man mistakenly conceives of God in corporeal form, but in another more profound way, which is as close as Maimonides gets to mysticism (not, however, that this is the only place where he exhibits mystical influence): "Matter," he says, "is a strong veil preventing the apprehension of that which is separate from matter as it truly is." Whenever our intellect attempts to apprehend God or one of the separate intellects, "there subsists this greal veil [matter] interposed," and to this have "all the books of the prophets" alluded in saying that "we are separated by a veil from God and that He is hidden from us by a heavy cloud."[27] Yet when he wishes to cite examples from the "books of the prophets," he can only quote from Psalms, and later, to be sure, from the Torah concerning the manifestation of God "in a thick cloud" at Sinai.

In fact, strange as it may appear, he may have intended by "all the prophets" not so much the Hebrew Bible as the Qur'ān, where the Arab unbelievers say concerning the revelation there is a veil (*hijāb*) between them and it (Sura 41.5), and that it is not possible to speak with God except by revelation "or from behind a veil" (Sura 42.51). According to the Muslim mystics, the *hijāb* in fact is a metaphor for the phenomena of the physical world which conceal the revelation of truth.[28]

Maimonides concludes this chapter with a rather startling statement, namely, that this manifestation of God described as "in a thick cloud" draws attention to the fact "that apprehension [*idrāk*] of His true reality is impossible for us because of the dark matter that encompasses *us* and not Him." Now, even if we could quarrel about the exact meaning of the Arabic term *mumtani*ᶜ here, which can mean "impossible" but also can mean simply "prevented, inaccessible," still it is clear that Maimonides means to say that our physical, corporeal form prevents or at least hinders the apprehension of God.

In a recent article, to which we shall refer in more detail, Shlomo Pines, the translator of the **Guide** into English, has cited this statement as proof that Maimonides either held that God is essentially unknowable, or that he cannot be grasped by the human intellect, which is dependent on sense perceptions and images. (Pines' insight there that this may be related to a theory of Ibn Bājja, which he discusses in detail, is intriguing but perhaps unprovable.) However, this would be strange indeed; for Maimonides throughout his writings, not just in the **Guide**, argues precisely that the apprehension of God and the knowledge of God is the ultimate perfection and end goal of man! Now we learn that this is, in fact, impossible.

Obviously, this is not the correct interpretation of the passage. The key lies in the understanding of two terms: *idrāk ḥaqīqata*, which really means "apprehension (or comprehension) in reality," and *mumtaniᶜ*, which we have already discussed as something ambiguous. In other words, the passage may better be understood to mean that "apprehension *in reality* is prevented to us (or hindered for us)" because of our physical nature, which is far different from saying that apprehension of God is impossible.

What Maimonides intends here, I believe, is that true comprehension of the reality of the essential nature of God is prevented because of the material nature of man. This does not, however, mean we cannot apprehend God at all. Indeed, he closes the chapter by saying that "near Him, may He be exalted, there is no darkness, but perpetual light the overflow of which illumines all that is dark." This "overflow," or emanation (Arabic *faiḍ*) is the key, for it is solely because of this, the emanation of the Active Intellect, that man is enabled to know anything. This is equally the source of man's apprehension and cognition and of prophetic revelation.[29]

In the previously cited article, Pines further says that *idrāk*, apprehension, of the Active Intellect as discussed by Maimonides does not necessarily mean "identity" with it (a better term would be "conjunction"). This is a complicated and highly technical aspect of philosophy which I do not wish to get into here at all, since it would require a lengthy discourse on Aristotle, Alexander of Aphrodisas, Al-Fārābī, and Averroes. However, Pines arrives at his conclusion chiefly on the basis of one passage in the **Guide** III.54, where Maimonides in fact is talking about the apprehension of *God*, not conjunction with the Active Intellect. His argument there is that the prophets as well as the philosophers have stated that the true end of man is the apprehension of God, and that in Hebrew the term wisdom (*ḥokhmah*) means only this. Further, that this apprehension means not only of God but of the actions which are attributed to him and which are to be imitated by man. Pines quite rightly says that, given the wording there and Maimonides' "views on the limits of man's cognition of Deity," apprehension of God does not mean "an intellectual act that brings about the identity of the subject and object of intellection." But Maimonides, in fact, does not identify the Active Intellect with God (or at least it is not clear that he does so), and thus Pines makes a weak argument.[30]

Of all the passages cited by Pines, he overlooked one which is the most important. In the previously cited passage in **Guide** I.1, where he says man posesses peculiarly the faculty of apprehension, Maimonides goes on to say "this apprehension was likened unto the apprehension of the deity...but only appears so to the first stirrings of opinion." It is because of this "divine intellect conjoined with man" that it was said of man that he is made in the image of God.[31] In other words, a man is *like* God in his intellectual apprehension, but not the *same* as God, as Maimonides later explains that God is at once both the subject of intellectual cognition and the object and the process all in one.

Indeed, in one of the passages which Pines himself cited, this becomes clearer. In **Guide** II.4 Maimonides observes that it is the Active Intellect which "brings into existence," that is causes to function, the intellect in man, and that this activated intellect in man derives from the overflow (or emanation), previously mentioned, of the Active Intellect which we apprehend. Nor, of course, does this occur to an equal degree in all men, but it is rather dependent on the level of perfection attained through moral and intellectual preparation. In only one place does Maimonides, in fact, say specifically that he *does* believe in union or conjunction with the Active Intellect, and this is only for the highest class of men who contemplate this more or less constantly.[32] There is yet one more passage where he comes very close to explicitly stating the doctrine of conjunction, and that is when he explains the allegorical meaning of such words as "to approach," "to touch," or "come near" with regard to God, all of which "signify the union of cognition with what is cognized," and this is the meaning of all such passages, "for nearness to Him, may He be exalted, consists in apprehending Him."[33]

Maimonides concludes the **Guide** with his famous parable, which he proudly tells us he "invented," but which, as I shall demonstrate ("Maimonides and Some Muslim Sources"), is actually derived chiefly from al-Fārābī and in part is also influenced by Ibn Bājja, of the ruler in his city and his subjects outside trying to get in. Some are able to get partly inside, others into the palace itself, and others to be in the presence of the king. Those who try to reach the palace but never enter it are the multitude who adhere to the Torah, "the ignoramuses who observe the commandments" (he means they only observe the commandments, but do not engage in philosophical study). Those who have attained perfection in study and metaphysics are with the ruler, and have attained the rank of prophet and even higher. One who "thinks and frequently mentions God, without knowledge, following a mere imagining" or a belief on the authority of someone else is altogether outside the palace. "If, however, you have apprehended God and His acts in accordance with what is required by the intellect" you must then strengthen "the bond between you and Him—that is, the intellect" by love of God, which is proportionate to the apprehension, and by worship (or service of God, Arabic *ᶜibāda*;cf. Hebrew *ᶜavodah*) which Maimonides says "consists in setting thought to work on the first intelligible." And so he concludes with an exhortation to his student that the intellect which overflows, or emanates, from God to man is the bond between us and him, and this bond can either be strengthened or weakened, as man chooses.[34]

The perfection of knowledge in man has as its consequence another, perhaps to our way of thinking more practical, goal than mere intellectual perfection and service of God. In **Guide** III.11 Maimonides states what is perhaps the most fitting conclusion for this paper, that the great evils which come about among human beings are due to the privation of knowledge, "all of them derive from ignorance." He compares this to blind men, who from absence of sight stumble and injure not only themselves but others, so "the various sects of men—every individual according to the extent of his ignorance—does to himself and to others great evils." But knowledge would prevent this, "for through cognition of the truth, enmity and hatred are removed and the inflicting of harm by people on one another is abolished." Thus, he says, Isaiah tells us that "They shall not hurt nor destroy in all My holy mountain; for the earth shall be full of the knowledge of the Lord" (Isaiah 11:9).[35] "Know this," Maimonides concludes; and significantly it is with this very quotation that he ended the **Mishneh Torah**, a code of law for Jews, but like his philosophical work, with implications reaching beyond his time and place to the entire world.

Notes

[1] There are, of course, a few casual references in the popular books on Jewish philosophy of David Neumark, Simeon Bernfeld, Julius Guttmann, Isaac Husik (the last two also available in English), and the more modern but no less popular works of George Vajda (e.g., *Introduction à la pensée juive du Moyen-Age* [Paris, 1947]) and Colette Sirat, *Jewish philosophical thought in the Middle Ages* (Hebrew) (Jerusalem, 1975) (her section on Maimonides is disappointing, showing no awareness of the research which has been done). One early attempt at such a study was Simon Rawidowicz, "Knowledge of God, a study in Maimonides' Philosophy of Religion," in *Ve-zot liyhudah* (Judah L. Landau jubilee volume) (Tel-Aviv, 1937), pp. 78-121 (English section), but it is unsatisfactory, not only in that it utilizes Hebrew and English translations of the **Guide** which are less than accurate, but that it is very general.

[2] See, e.g., Harry A. Wolfson, "The Aristotelian Predicables and Maimonides' Division of Attributes," in *Essays and Studies in Memory of Linda R. Miller*, ed. Israel Davidson (N.Y., 1938), pp. 201-34; idem., "Maimonides on Negative Attributes," in *Louis Ginzberg Jubilee Volume* (N.Y., 1945) I, 411-46 (both significant articles, much more satisfactory than some of his later work), and of some interest is Julius Guttmann, "*Torat ha-elohim shel ha-Rambam*" (Hebrew) in *Essays in honour of...J.H. Hertz*, ed. I. Epstein, et al. (London, 1942), pp. 53-69 (note especially pp. 61-62 and the note there where he deals with previous criticism).

[3] Franz Rosenthal, *Knowledge Triumphant* (Leiden, 1970), pp 95-96 and cf. p. 78. The standard English translation of this passage from "Book of Knowledge" may readily be consulted as reprinted in Isadore Twersky, ed., *A Maimonides Reader* (Phila., 1972), p. 46 (it is incorrectly translated, as are almost all the sections reprinted in that book). There is a new English translation, **The Book of Knowledge**, tr. H.M. Russell and J. Weinberg (Edinburgh, 1981) (see p. 6 there) which is somewhat better, but still not entirely correct.

[4] See below, p. 100

[5] **Guide** (Arabic *Dalālat al-ḥa'irīn*, ed. Issachar Joel [Jerusalem, 1931], p. 112), tr. Shlomo Pines (Chicago, 1963) I. 68, p. 163. Future references will be to Pines' translation, with the understanding that I have checked all citations in Joel's Arabic text (the more recent Judeo-Arabic edition by Joseph Kafiḥ is no improvement at all on Joel's text).

[6] Translator's introduction, **Guide**, pp. xcvii and liii.

[7] **Mishneh Torah** (Rome, 1490; photo rpt. Jerusalem, 1955), pp. 692-93; Constantinople, 1509; photo rpt. Jerusalem, 1972, vol. IV). The section appears, incorrectly translated (by Twersky himself?), in *Maimonides Reader*, pp. 226-27.

[8] Pines' translation, p. 139. The **Eight Chapters** is cited in the critical edition with English translation by Joseph Gorfinkle (N.Y., 1912), pp. 100-01. See selections from this translation rpt. in Twersky, *Maimonides Reader*, where this section appears on p. 385.

[9] P. 102.

[10] **Guide**, p. 482. For the probable identity of the philosophers to whom Maimonides refers, see Wolfson, "Maimonides on Negative Attributes," p. 415.

[11] *Loc. cit* For the meaning of "equivocal" or "amphibolous" terms (referred to throughout the *Guide*), see **Maimonides' Treatise on Logic**, ed. with English translation Israel Efros (N.Y., 1938), p. 60 (translation), and Harry A. Wolfson, "The Amphibolous Terms in Aristotle, Arabic Philosophy and Maimonides," *Harvard Theological Review* 31 (1938): 151-73, especially pp. 164-66.

[12] **Guide**, p. 483. This subject requires fuller treatment, of course.

[13] **Guide** I. 68, p. 163; cf. the very excellent explanation in the medieval Hebrew commentary of Shem Tov b. Joseph Ibn Shem Tov in the editions of the Hebrew translation (**Moreh Nevukhim**) by Ibn Tibbon. The Aristotelian background here will be found in *De Anima* III and IV.

[14] **Mishneh Torah**, "Book of Knowledge," "Foundations of the Torah" 1.1.

[15] P. 74; cf. David Kaufmann, *Die Spuren des al-Bataljusis* (Budapest, 1880; photo rpt. Gregg International, 1972), pp. 39-40.

[16] **Guide** I. 34, p. 75. (Pines' error in translation here is surprising, for it is not just a matter of interpretation of a word, always open to question, but actually of grammatical usage.)

[17] Tr. Gorfinkle, p. 101, and see his note to the Hebrew text, p. 54 (not "55"), n. 37.

[18] See my discussion of this in "Attaining 'Happiness' (*Eudaimonia*) in Medieval Muslim and Jewish Philosophy," *Centerpoint* 4 (1981): 26.

[19] **Guide**, p. 78. Again, the precise meaning of the Arabic is important here; *bi-naṣṣ kitāb* does not just mean "by [means of] a text of a book," but rather *kitāb* is used here in its very common Jewish meaning of "scripture," and refers in fact to Isaiah 3.3 (Pines neglected even to give the source of the quotation); cf. Munk's note in his French translation of **Guide** here: "par le texte d'un livre (sacré)," and al-Ḥarizi's Hebrew translation, "*mi-divrey ha-katuv*," referring to the citation from Isaiah.

[20] **Guide** I. 46, pp. 98-99.

[21] **Guide** I. 35, p. 81 (concerning what he says there about the difficulty of the interpretation of texts, that he should be told "The interpretation of this text is understood by men of knowledge," cf. Ibn Rushd, *On the Harmony of Religion and Philosophy*, tr. George Hourani (London, 1961,) p. 60 and n. 138.

[22] **Guide** I. 49, p. 109. On angels in the thought of Ibn Sīnā , see his "On the Proof of Prophecies" tr. Michael Marmura in Ralph Lerner and Muhsin Mahdi, eds., *Medieval Political Philosophy* (Ithaca, N.Y., 1972), pp. 115, 118. On the identification of angels with the separate intelligences in al-Rāzī's commentary on Ibn Sīnā's *ᶜUyūn al-ḥikma*, see F. Rahman, "The Eternity of the World and the Heavenly Bodies in Post-Avicennan Philosophy," in George F. Hourani, ed., *Essays on Islamic Philosophy and Science* (Albany, 1975), p. 224.

[23] **Mishnah ᶜim peirush Mosheh ben Maimon, Zeraᶜim**, ed.

Joseph Kafiḥ (Jerusalem, 1963), pp. 41-42; my translation of this hitherto untranslated text; cf. also **Mishneh Torah**, "Book of Knowledge," "Foundations of the Torah" 4.8.

[24] **Guide** I. 51, p. 113; ibid. I.1, p. 23; cf. the discussion in my "Attaining Happiness," p. 24.

[25] There is, incidentally, no doubt whatever that Ibn Shem Tov was right in explaining this as the acquired intellect and not the active intellect, though he considered that possibility, because of the previously cited passage (p. 190) where Maimonides specifically says it is the acquired intellect—although Ibn Shem Tov does not mention that in his commentary. Maimonides undoubtedly derived these ideas from Ibn Sīnā, who said: "There exists in man a faculty by which he is differentiated from the rest of animals and other things. This is called the rational soul," and this is the material intellect ("On the Proof of Prophecies," previously cited, p. 113); cf. also Aristotle *Meta.* 1072b 24 and *N.E.* 1174b 21.

[26] **Guide** III.23, pp. 492-93. Cf. also *Guide* III.12, p. 446.

[27] III.9, pp. 436-7. Also in *Peraqim be-haṣlaḥah*, erroneously ascribed to Maimonides, the treatise commences: "Perhaps when your heart becomes clear [untroubled] and the clouds are separated from it...," which W.Z. Bacher correctly explained as the clouds of sensuality, which interfere with the true knowledge of God ("Treatise on Eternal Bliss Attributed to Moses Maimūni," *Jewish Quarterly Review* [o.s.] 9 [1897]: 271). The text of this almost entirely ignored treatise may be found in Moses b. Maimon, **Qoveṣ teshuvot** (Leipzig, 1859; photo rpt. Westmead, England, 1969), II. 32, and in a critical edition, ed. H.S. Davidowitz and D.H. Baneth (Jerusalem, 1939), text and Hebrew tr., p. 3. The Christian theologian Gregory of Nyssa may be another source for comparison. See also above, "Maimonides' Impact on World Culture," p. 17, the quotation from the introduction to his commentary on the Mishnah where the same Arabic word *ḥijab*, "veil" is used.

[28] See generaly the article "Hi*dj*āb" in *Shorter Encyclopedia of Islam*. The works of Ibn Sīnā and even al-Ghazālī should be examined also.

[29] This is a subject which itself deserves a complete study; cf. **Guide**, pp. 24, 258, 275, 277ff., 279 (definition), 347, 369-70, 373ff., 377, 471, 474, 475.

[30] Pines, "The Limitations of Human Knowledge According to Al-Farabi, ibn Bajja, and Maimonides," in Isadore Twersky, ed., *Studies in Medieval Jewish History and Literature* (Cambridge, Mass., 1979), p. 91. The passages in *Guide* to which he refers are pp. 152, 258, 636, 638 (he means surely p. 637).

[31] **Guide**, p. 23.

[32] **Guide** III.8, p. 432; cf. also II. 36, p. 369 and II. 38, p. 377.

[33] **Guide** I. 18, p. 43. It is strange that these passages were overlooked by Pines.

[34] **Guide** III. 51, pp. 620-21. See my discussion of the parable in "Maimonides and Some Muslim Sources," p. 98 below.

[35] **Guide**, pp. 440-41.

Maimonides and Some Muslim Sources: al-Fārābī, Ibn Sinā, Ibn Rushd

(Symposium on Maimonides
University of Southern California,
March 27-28, 1985)

Scholarship on Maimonides has been, to say the least, erratic. The medieval commentators on the **Guide** often had a better understanding of the real meaning of his thought than do many modern scholars.[1] After the Middle Ages, nothing of significance was done on Maimonides until the last century (if we discount the analysis of the **Guide** by Leibniz).[2] In spite of a proliferation of studies, chiefly articles, in this century, there remains surprisingly little really solid work.

As already indicated (see above, "Maimonides' Impact on World Culture"), the careful student of Maimonides must become familiar with all of his work, not just the obviously philosophical.

Similarly, students of Maimonides (in fact, of medieval Jewish philosophy in general) must be at home also in Muslim philosophy and culture. It remains a fact, however, that very little work has been done on the relation of Maimonides to his Arabic sources.[3] The number of such articles is altogether very insignificant, and it is a measure of the status of one of our colleagues at this symposium, Herbert Davidson, that he is the author of at least two of the best of these (one, to be sure, dealing with Maimonides' "Eight Chapters" rather than the **Guide**, but it is so perceptive that it should be required reading for anyone who studies Maimonides seriously.)

Maimonides' position as a student and friend of Muslim scholars during his formative years in Spain is well known. For instance, he himself states that he knew the son of the great astronomer and mathematician of Seville Jābir Ibn Aflaḥ (although he appears not to have read, or even to have known the nature of Ibn Aflaḥ's book which in fact criticizes Ptolemy and certainly does not agree with him, as Maimonides wrongly states in **Guide** II.9). He also studied with one of the students of the Spanish Muslim philosoher Ibn Bājja.[4] Maimonides praised Ibn Bājja in his famous letter to Samuel Ibn Tibbon, and cites him in the **Guide**. His references to other Muslim philosophers, such as al-Fārābī and Averroes, and are well known.

The purpose of this paper is certainly not to fill the gap in our knowledge of Maimonides' sources in Muslim philosophy. Before any definitive study can be undertaken, we need many more specialized analyses of particular topics and philosophers, as well as linguistic studies (by which I mean a comparison of Maimonides' Arabic terminology with that of his sources), which has not yet been attempted at all. What I hope to do is suggest possible areas of influence, using only a few topics as illustration, or at least points of interesting similarity, between Maimonides and three of his predecessors in Muslim thought: al-Fārābī, Ibn Sīnā (Avicenna) and Ibn Rushd (Averroes).

One of the most striking metaphors in the **Guide** is the comparison of esoteric knowledge and prophetic truth to flashes of lightning in a dark night. To some, these flashes come constantly; this is the level of Moses. Others receive such a flash only once, and these are they who prophesy only once. Still others receive flashes at irregular intervals; the majority of the prophets. Finally, some receive no flash at all, but only a kind of reflected light, and even that is not constant.

There is no difference whatever between the prophet and the philosopher; indeed, the philosopher is on a higher level than the mere prophet (Abraham Heschel's article of many years ago in which he posed the question, "Did Maimonides think he had attained the level of prophecy?" needs to be answered negatively, for he surely believed that he had reached a *higher* level). Anyone who reveals esoteric knowledge, by whatever means, is a prophet.[5] Pines, indeed, was greatly confused by this, and having correctly explained that those who see the lightning flashes may be equated with possessors of "intuitive theoretical knowledge," he states that according to Maimonides only Moses had this to a perfect degree, and quite correctly suggests that this "might mean" that Moses is to be regarded as the supreme philosopher.[6] It is not, as Pines thought, that all men who receive lightning flashes are prophets, but that all such possess intuitive knowledge to a greater or lesser degree depending on their rational and moral perfection.

The origin of the lightning flashes metaphor may be sought ultimately in the fifth-century Christian mystic Pseudo-Dionysius and his apparent influence on the ninth-century founder of Sufism, D͟hu'l-Nūn al-Miṣrī.[7] While the possible influence of mystical ideas, particularly Ṣūfī, al-G͟hazālī and even Jewish mysticism, upon Maimonides has scarcely been considered (one might say, not at all), there is a more proximate source for these ideas of lightning flashes and prophecy for Maimonides. Ibn Sīnā certainly played a far more important role as a source of Maimonides than I think has hereto been realized. One of his works, which has been completely ignored by Jewish scholars, is "On the proof of prophecies" (*Fī it͟hbāt al- nubuwwāt*). The striking similarity of this treatise to many of Maimonides' ideas can hardly escape notice.

Here, he cites Qur'ān XXIV.35 concerning Allāh as light, and the statement that he "guides to his light whom he will" (*nūrihī* in this verse is ambiguous and can either mean Allāh's light or the light of the believer; many commentaries have discussed this).[8] It is interesting that in the continuation of that Sūra, reference is made to God's lightning: "wellnigh the gleam of his lightning snatches away the sight."

Ibn Sīnā says that light is an equivocal term[9], with an "essential" and a "metaphorical" meaning, and here it is metaphorical for the good and that which leads to the good. The "niche" to which the light is compared (as a lamp standing in a niche) is the material intellect; which is to say, as he previously explains, the intellect in potentiality, ready to receive impressions of the universal forms. The light is the actualized intellect.[10] In one of his more mystical statements in another work, *Is͟hārāt*[11], he explains that the mystic, like the philosopher, must advance through various stages of preparation until he reaches a certain level when glimpses of the light are revealed, like flashes of lightning which appear and disappear; "moments" (*awqāt*). The frequency of these increases until they become more or less regular and the flashes become flames of (permanent) light.

Having seen that Maimonides, like Ibn Sīnā, equates the revelation of esoteric knowledge with the flashes of revelation to the prophet, we can now understand his allusion in the dedication of his work to his student, Joseph b. Judah Ibn Shimᶜon of Ceuta (and not, of course, Ibn ᶜAqnin of Barcelona, as is still often said). He says to him that when he became convinced that he (Joseph) had acquired a certain proficiency in mathematics, astronomy and science, "I began to let you see certain flashes" of the secrets of prophetic books.

Then, in his general introduction, he states a very peculiar thing. It has already been noted that Maimonides, elsewhere the very model of clear writing and lucid explanation, is exceedingly obscure in the **Guide**. Here, he admits this; indeed, promises it, stating he shall only set down "chapter headings" (summaries) of his ideas. "For my purpose is that the truths be glimpsed and then again be concealed." The real truths, he says, are to be concealed from the "vulgar among the people."[12] Even one perfect in knowledge cannot fully explain the truths he understands, for when he wishes to do so the subject "will appear, flash, and then be hidden again."[13]

He returns again and again to the danger of expounding esoteric knowledge. This applies not only to philosophy and prophecy, but also to natural science in some respects.[14] Such knowledge is hidden from the masses not because of its danger, but because the "intellect is incapable of receiving them; only flashes of them are made to appear" to those properly prepared, as he states later in the **Guide**.[15]

After giving examples of esoteric knowledge which can only be explained as he earlier has said in "chapter headings," such as the attributes of God, he says that certain things are nevertheless necessary knowledge for all, such as the incorporeality of God. If someone does not understand these ideas and supporting texts, he must be told that their interpretation is known by men of knowledge.[16]

Similarly, Ibn Sīnā said that the prophet is necessary for giving laws and to let men know what they must about the oneness of God, obedience to him, etc. "But [the prophet] ought not to involve [people] with doctrines pertaining to the knowledge of God" (i.e., knowledge about the essence and existence of God), for this will simply confuse the religion (*dīn*) of the masses.[17] "Nor is it proper for any man to reveal that he possesses knowledge he is hiding from the vulgar." This reminds us in a striking way of Maimonides' repeated statements about the "vulgar," "ignoramuses," etc.

Again, in his "On the proof of prophecies," Ibn Sīnā explains that the Greek philosophers hid their secret doctrine in symbols and parables. So Averroes (Ibn Rushd) argued that certain difficulties can only be understood by the elite, and the masses must take them at their apparent meaning. Maimonides also says that there is no excuse for anyone not accepting the authority of speculative scholars about something which he himself is incapable of understanding. Was he influenced in this by Averroes' quite similar opinions?

Esoteric knowledge, however, was not something which fascinated the philosophers for its own sake, even acknowledging the important influence of mysticism on Ibn Sīnā and perhaps, if to a lesser degree, Maimonides himself. It was necessary not only to conceal from the masses and the "vulgar" ideas which were too complicated for them to grasp, but also to conceal dangerous ideas and opinions which were in apparent conflict with religious doctrines. We have already learned from Leo Strauss something of this, but the truth goes far beyond even the outlines which he sketched. It is impossible to grasp the extent of what could be considered heretical ideas in Maimonides' writing without constantly being on guard against taking almost anything at face value. Difficult as it may be for some of the more religiously inclined Jewish scholars of today to understand, much less accept, some of Maimonides' ideas, yet there is almost nothing original in these heretical views in Maimonides. He certainly did not consider himself a heretic, nor necessarily as breaking new ground in what he wrote. His passionate quest for truth in all things led him to a reasoned acceptance of the conclusions reached by Greek and Muslim philosophers before him.

There is no question of a "conflict" of religion and philosophy, of reason and revelation, as poorly informed students of medieval Scholasticism have so long wished to transfer these notions to Muslim and Jewish thought. There can be only one truth, as there is only one source of truth, and not many "little truths" (to borrow Santayana's term). What prophetic revelation brings in the way of flashes of light to the masses, the philosopher sees in the full blaze of rational illumination.

Now, imagination, as is known, is the source of prophecy according to Maimonides. The imaginative faculty, though it is produced by "overflow" from the Active Intellect like the rational faculty, is nevertheless "not the act of the intellect but rather its contrary," for it does not differentiate and abstract like the intellect.

Imagination is the source not only of prophecy but of dreams, which are like prophecy. This, too, is not original with Maimonides, but goes back to Aristotle. Indeed, it may be of some value to quote here an interesting statement attributed to Aristotle in a fragment preserved in Sextus Empiricus:

> Aristotle said that the conception of the gods arose among mankind from two sources, namely, from events which affect the soul and from the phenomena of the heavens. It arose from events which affect the soul because of the things that occur in sleep, i.e., its inspirations and its prophecies...[18]

According to al-Fārābī, too, imagination (*phantasia*) is not solely dependent on the memory and senses, but also consists of an activity, mostly in sleep, called *mimesis* (imitation). This "creative" imagination provides access to metaphysical truth with the help of symbols. Prophets then have a superior power of creative *phantasia*, and also a particularly powerful intellect which has reached the highest attainment of knowledge of which humans are capable.

Ibn Sīnā, on the other hand, held that the perfected rational man *is* the prophet, the highest level of philosophy being prophecy. It is the overflow of the highest knowledge to imagination which builds up the symbols of truth.[19]

Now, it is somewhat astonishing to find Maimonides saying that imagination is also in true reality the evil impulse. For every deficiency of reason or character is due to the action of the imagination, or consequent upon its action.[20]

Al-Fārābī has made a very similar statement in a treatise which we know was seen by Maimonides, "The Political regime" (*al-Siyāsāt al-madanīyah*); namely, that whenever man is misled by his appetitive faculty, in desiring some other good than the ultimate (which is rational perfection), "then everything that originates from him is evil."[21]

Thus, imagination, which is the source of prophecy, is not held in very high regard by Maimonides. In fact, prophecy is held altogether in rather low esteem, and regarded even less than in some of the Arabic sources. Part of this, as I have written elsewhere, may be connected with polemical issues directed at Islam, but certainly not all of it can be explained thus. On the other hand, there are gradations within the ranks of prophets, as he makes clear more than once. Perhaps the more important statement on this—which surely cannot be understood at all without a knowledge of his Muslim source here—is in **Guide** II.37 where he distinguishes three classes of people: those to whom the intellectual overflow reaches only the rational, but not the imaginative, faculty. These are the speculative scholars. The second is that to whom the overflow reaches both rational and imaginative faculties, and if the imaginative faculty "is in a state of ultimate perfection owing to its natural disposition," this is the class of the prophets. The third is that to whom the overflow reaches *only* the imaginative faculty, and these are rulers of cities, soothsayers, and the like.[22]

We may surely see Ibn Sīnā behind these views, at least partially, for he held that the prophet has an extraordinary capacity for intuitive knowledge, by which he unites with the Active Intellect. His faculty of imagination is thus perfect, which allows the prophetic use of imagery and metaphors. The forms of the Active Intellect become imprinted on his soul (*illhām*, literally "to gulp down," this is the individual revelation or self-instruction). General revelation, *waḥy*, to others, may result from this, but it does not require intellectual perfection which *ilhām* does.[23] This is doubtless what Maimonides means when he says that sometimes the overflow has no other result than to render the individual prophet perfect, and at other times it compels him to address people and let the overflow reach them.[24] Not only did Maimonides, probably, utiize these statements of Ibn Sīnā, they also influenced Judah ha-Levy, who literally quotes part of the above in his *Kuzari*.[25]

There is, however, an apparent problem of a very serious nature, for Maimonides states that the imaginative faculty did not enter into the prophecy of Moses at all, for the intellect overflowed to him without the intermediation of imagination. This would appear to put Moses in the class of mere speculative scholars, to whom the overflow reaches only the rational, but not the imaginative, faculty.

Elsewhere, Maimonides has stated that he does not intend to talk about Moses at all in the **Guide**, but this is one of the many statements where he contradicts himself. There, he merely calls attention to his previous distinction between Moses and other prophets (in his commentary on the *mishnah* of *Sanhedrin*, "*Ḥeleq*," and in his **Code**, laws of the foundation of the Torah),[26] and says that all his statements about prophecy in the **Guide** refer to other prophets.

The solution to the dilemma appears in II.38, where he states that while the overflow perfects the imaginative faculty of the prophet, it is the same overflow which perfects the rational faculty—indeed, more so, for the overflow truly goes to the rational faculty. He then makes the very strong assertion that only one who achieves *speculative* perfection is able to apprehend objects of knowledge when there is an overflow of the Active Intellect to him.[27] Moses possessed such a perfection in a unique degree, so that his apprehension "necessarily" resulted in, not a revelation, but a "call to *law*," which no other prophet before or after him had.

In other words, Moses is made the *supreme ruler* in Maimonides' view, and there is no doubt that he was influenced in all this by al-Fārābī, who stated that the supreme ruler·is he who has acquired perfection in knowledge, and all the necessary qualities of a supreme ruler are found "only in the one who possesses great and superior natural dispositions, when his soul is in union with the Active Intellect." It is only of him that it should be said that he receives (true) revelation.[28]

This is apparently also the explanation of the difficult statement in III.51 that some may achieve a state where their intellect is constantly turned toward God even while pursuing bodily matters or talking to people, and that this is the rank, not of *all* the prophets, but of Moses and also the Patriachs. He must mean here also the rank of Moses as a leader and ruler.

This is incidentally, why Maimonides elsewhere stated that it is necessary for the ruler of a city (or state), *if he is a prophet*, to imitate the perceived attributes of God in order to rule justly.[29]

These ideas of al-Fārābī and Ibn Sīnā underlie the whole of **Guide** II.40, where Maimonides discusses the nature of society, rulers and laws. He begins with the remark that it has been clearly explained that man is political by nature, and in this he is not like other animals. The source for this is, of course, Aristotle.[30] Marcus Aurelius also said: "It was long ago made clear that we were born for fellowship. Is it not that the lower exist for the sake of the higher, and the higher for one another's sake?"[31] The best statement I have found on the subject is that of the sixteenth-century jurist and Christian Hebraist Hugo Grotius: "But among the traits characteristic of man is an impelling desire for society, not of any sort, but peaceful, and organized according to the measure of his intelligence, with those who are of his own kind."

Similary, al-Fārābī prefaced his above-cited remarks by saying that man belongs to a species that can only best accomplish its affairs in society. Ibn Sīnā put it that man differs from other animals in that he must live in association to benefit from others. These reciprocal transactions demand law and justice.

If imagination is the source of insight and revelation for the prophet, knowledge is the quest of the rational speculative being. Maimonides is very clear on the difference between *belief* (or, perhaps better, "conviction")[32] and *certain knowledge* concerning God, his attributes, etc. Belief is that which is represented, or impressed, upon the mind, with the affirmation that it corresponds to reality outside the mind. If there is further a conviction that no other belief is possible, this is certain knowledge.[33] Stubbornness is not what is intended here, for he mentions being one of those whose aspiration is to attain the highest rank of speculation and gain certain knowledge of God's being. Thus, what is required is perseverance in perfecting the intellect to reach this level.

In his famous parable, of which he proudly states "I invented it," of the citizens of the city around the ruler's palace, some are said to hold incorrect opinions, others are the multitude of ignoramuses who observe the commandments of the Law (without thinking about or understanding it), and others have true opinions but only on the basis of authority, and some have "plunged into speculation" and achieved knowledge or the demonstration of everything that is subject to demonstration, and so have "come close to certainty."[34]

Al-Fārābī appears to be the source for all of this. In "Attainment of Happiness" he says: "The attainment of certain truth is aimed at in every problem. Yet frequently we do not attain certainty" except about a part of what is sought, and belief and persuasion about the rest.[35]

Now, Maimonides does not say it is necessary to *know* everything with certainty, only to have understood the demonstration of what can be demonstrated. This, too, is based on al-Fārābīs ideas as expressed in his *Commentary on Aristotle's Prior Analytics*; that it is not necessary to seek exactness in everything to the same extent, for in some things one can limit oneself to knowledge that is without absolute certainty but only demonstration.[36] (I shoud mention, incidentally, that the last two mentioned works of al-Fārābī have been available in English translation, one for many years and the other for several, yet they have scarcely been consulted by scholars.)

Nor can we allow Maimonides to escape entirely with full credit for his aforementioned parable, which, if original to an extent, is clearly based on al-Fārābī's enumeration of the ranks of the city, their duties and their abilities to comprehend.[37] (Of course, Ibn Bājja was also a major influence on this chapter of **Guide**, as already recognized by Profiat Duran in his commentary.)

Another area which demands more attention than it has received concerns Maimonides' views on attributes. While there has been, of course, some discussion of the famous doctrine of negative attributes, as far as I am aware practically nothing has been said about his statements on essence and existence. Particularly important is the observation that God has a necessary existence while everything else has merely a possible existence.[38] Now, apparently the source for this is not Aristotle, but Ibn Sīnā. I confess to finding myself very much one of the "perplexed" when it comes to trying to follow Ibn Sīnā in this, much less to sort out the arguments as to the originality of his contributions to what Aristotle already said. This has been a major subject of discussion among scholars of Muslim philosophy, again without arousing much interest among Jewish scholars. Nevertheless, it appears that he is the source of these views, and the connection with Maimonides is surely an area worth further study.[39] Incidentally, Pines' objection (p.135) that Maimonides says in the same sentence that he has "already demonstrated" and yet shall later demonstrate the same thing, and thus is inconsistent, is simply wrong. What Maimonides means—and, in fact, what he says—is that the necessary existence of God *has* been demonstrated (he means at I.52; p.117), and that there is no composition in God's nature *will* be demonstrated. They are two different arguments.

One of the most important statements which he makes concerning the nature of God, and which is very difficult to understand in that it apparently contradicts his repeated denial of assigning attributes to God, is that God is the *intellect* and the "intellectually cognizing *subject*" (as Pines somewhat incorrectly translates; the Arabic is *ᶜaqīl*, cf. Greek *nous* and *noē*; hence, the *process* of intellecting), and the intellectual *object* all in one.[40] He gives this as a "dictum of the philosophers," without—as usual with him—saying who, nor does Pines offer any but the most vague of explanations that it is found in Aristotle's *Metaphysics*. It is found, more or less, in Meta. *Lambda* 1074b.15 ff., where the activity of the so-called "divine intelligence" is said to be thought thinking itself (cf. also 1072b.20). Something similar is found in *De Anima*, where the "causal mental force" is said to be a faculty which knows itself by its own agency and is identical with the object of knowledge (III.6, 430b.24; III.7, 431a.1). As Maimonides says, all of this he has also "mentioned" in the Code of Law.[41] There he more than "mentions" it, but establishes it as a law, something which is required even for the masses to know, as one of what he calls the "foundations of the Torah." This is what he says:

> The Holy One, blessed be He, recognizes his true [essence] and knows it as it is, and he does not know with a knowledge which is external to himself, as we know. For our knowledge and ourselves are not one, but the Creator, blessed be he, he and his knowledge and his life are one from every aspect; for if he lived and knew with a knowledge separate from himself, there would be many deities: he, and his life, and his knowledge. But the thing is not so, rather [he is] one from every aspect of unity. You must say he is the knower, and he is the known, and he is the knowledge itself, everything in one. This thing there is no power in the mouth to utter it, nor in the ear to hear it, nor in the heart of man to recognize it clearly...

These ideas are much more fully elucidated by Maimonides in his **Eight Chapters on Ethics.**

Since we thus see that this is considered by Maimonides more than a passing notion, but a fundamental principle, it is important to look further into possible sources which may have influenced him on this.

One of these, even indirectly, must be Plotinus, who said:

> In the Intellectual-Principle itself [i.e., God], there is complete identity of Knower and Known...not by way of domiciliation [i.e., apparently, the intellect residing in the object of knowledge]...but by Essence [no distinction exists between Being and Knowing].[42]

Although he is too late to be considered a source, the great Ṣūfī of Spain Ibn al-ᶜArabī (born in 1165) also said: "Knowledge, the object known, and the knower are three to be considered one."[43]. Similar ideas are to be found in al-Fārābī and in Averroes.

Not all Muslims accepted this notion, of course. The orthodox Asharites strongly rejected it, and al-Ashᶜārī himself complained of Abu'l-Hudayal of the heretical Jahmiyyah (who denied all attributes but identified references in the Qur'ān to Allāh's knowledge with Allāh himself) that he thinks Allāh's knowledge is Allāh and that Allāh is knowledge.[44]

Al-Ghazālī also strongly attacked the Peripatetic identification of God's knowledge and essence in his *Tahāfut*.

In addition to holding God's knowledge to be identical with his essence, Maimonides also states his opinion that God's will is equally identical with his essence.[45] Without wishing to suggest that Averroes is necessarily the source for this, for it may be that Maimonides never saw the *Tahāfut al-tahāfut*, it is interesting to compare what Averroes says there. He argues that, apparently, will is an indication of a lack of the thing willed, and God has no lack. Also, it is a passive quality and a change, which do not apply either to God.[46] However, God's will is totally different from human will, as his knowledge is totally different from human knowledge.[47] God has knowledge of two opposites and brings into act only one of the two, and in this sense one may speak of God's will.

So, too, when Maimonides says that God wills the universe to exist, continually endowing it with permanence by his overflow, this is remarkably in accord with Averroes, who explains that God is not himself one of the four causes, but the *agent* of these causes, "drawing forth the universe from non-existence to existence and conserving it."[48]

As Fackenheim has already noted, al-Fārābī similarly

explained that "creation" is to be understood as the "preservation of the eternal existence of that thing whose existence is not *per se* eternally lasting."[49] Such apparently innocuous statements, though they could be brought into seeming harmony with certain sayings of the rabbis, are really a very far cry from any traditional notion of creation *ex nihilo*, itself a concept borrowed by Jewish writers (Sa^{c}adyah Gaon of the tenth century is the earliest source I can find) from Christian theology.

It is well known, or at least it used to be well known to medieval commentators on Maimonides, and perhaps less so today, that on such subjects as creation, immortality, eternality of the world, and resurrection, Maimonides held positions which were not in accord with apparent traditional Jewish teaching. Commentators used to write cryptically concerning these things, "*yesh bo sod*"—there is a secret, or esoteric meaning (following the example in this set by Maimonides himself).

Certainly when we come to investigate any of these topics in the thought of Maimonides it will not do to have recourse to pious wishful thinking, as was the case many years ago when Isaiah Sonne apparently silenced for all time the fruitful work that was being done in investigating the probably forged Maimonides treatise on resurrection. Not only this, but many of the so-called "letters" of Maimonides are partly or wholly forgeries. Careful analysis of the text is, of course, essential; but so also is a thorough investigation of the sources definitely and likely used by Maimonides. The extent to which this has been done so far, whether with Greek philosophical and scientific sources or with Muslim sources, is disappointing to the point of being scandalous.

It is to be hoped that as we commemorate the eight-hundred-and-fiftieth anniversary of Maimonides, the time has finally come to begin a serious and hopefully even a cooperative effort to undertake this investigation.

Such a cooperative venture must involve not only Jewish scholars in many countries, but scholars of Muslim and Greek philosophy as well. The task is too enormous for any one person or even group of persons to accomplish alone. Certainly there could be no more fitting tribute to the memory of him of whom it was said "From Moses to Moses there never arose one like Moses" than to dedicate this year to such a beginning.

Notes

[1] I was happy to see that this view is also shared by Jacob Becker, *Sodo shel 'Moreh Nevukhim'* (p. 25)—the only significant study in Hebrew, aside from Even-Shmuel's almost totally neglected commentary in his edition.

[2] Cf. Lenn E. Goodman, "Maimonides and Leibniz," *Journal of Jewish Studies* 31 (1980): 214-36. Leibniz' commentary is reprinted in Buxtorf's Latin translation of the *Guide, Doctor perplexorum* (Basle, 1629; photo rpt. Westmead, England, 1966).

[3] *Ibn Bajjah ve-ha-Rambam* (published, Jerusalem, 1959. Hebrew, with English summary.); Emil Fackenheim, "The Possibility of the Universe in Al-Farabi, Ibn Sina and Maimonides," *American Academy for Jewish Research Proceedings (PAAJR)* 16 (1946-7): 39-70 (especially p. 57 ff.; Fackenheim's study, while useful, is marred by some problems, such as his acceptance of the "Treatise on Resurrection" as a genuine work); S. Nirenstein, "The Problem of the Existence of God in Maimonides, Alanus and Averroes," *J.Q.R.* (n.s.) 14 (1923-24): 395-545 (an important article); Leo Strauss, "Science politique de Maimonides et de Farabi," *R.E.J.* 100 *bis* (1936): 1-37; Harry A. Wolfson, "Amphibolous Terms in Artistotle, Arabic Philosophy and Maimonides," *Harvard Theological Review* 31 (1938): 151-73; Herbert Davidson, "Maimonides' Shemoneh Peraqim and Alfarabi's *Fusal al-Madani*," *PAAJR* 31 (1963): 33-50; Harry Blumberg, "Al-Farabi, Ibn Bajja and Maimonides on the Solitary Life" (Hebrew), *Sinai* 78 (1976): 135-45; M. Stern, "Alghazali, Maimonides and Ibn Paquda on Repentance," *Journal of the American Academy of Religion* 47 (1979): 589-607 (not a very useful article); Harry Blumberg, "The Problem of Immortality in Avicenna, Maimonides and St. Thomas Aquinas," *Harry A. Wolfson Jubilee Volume* (Jerusalem, 1965) I, 165-85; Joel Kraemer, "Alfarabi's *Opinions of the Virtuous City* and Maimonides' *Foundations of the Law*," *Studia orientalia memoriae D.H. Baneth* (Jerusalem, 1979), pp. 107-53 (a correct argument which could be summarized in a

couple of sentences instead of many pages). Davidson's other very important article alluded to, though not directly dealing with Maimonides, is "Arguments from the Concept of Particularization in Arabic Philosophy," *Between East and West* 18 (1968): 399-314. While Jacob Dienstag's listing of sources used by Maimonides, introduction to his (edited) collected *Studies in Maimonides and St. Thomas Aquinas* (N.Y., 1975), is of some help, there are many important bibliographical omissions and several erroneous statements.

[4] See **Guide** II.9; cf. Even-Shmuel's edition, **Moreh nevukhim** (Jerusalem, 1949) II, 1, p. 134, n.7. Maimonides' letter to Ibn Tibbon in the critical edition of A. Marx in *J.Q.R.* (n.s.) 25:379.

[5] **Guide of the Perplexed**, tr. Shlomo Pines (Chicago, 1963), pp. 7, 360-61, 363, 370; cf. Abravanel's (Hebrew) commentary to the introduction to the **Guide**.

[6] Pines' introduction to **Guide**, p. cv.

[7] Pseudo-Dionysius, *Angelica Hierarchia*, or *De caelesti hierarchia* (*P.G.* 3); cf., e.g., J.-Th. Welter, *L'exemplum dans la littérature réligieuse du moyen âge* (1927), p. 321, and see Adalbert Merx, *Idee und Grundlinien einer allgemeiner Geschichte der Mystik* (Heidelberg, 1893), p. 18 ff., also on the Ṣūfī Dhu'l-Nūn al-Miṣrī, and cf. Reynold A. Nicholson, *A Literary History of the Arabs* (Cambridge, 1956), p. 386 ff., and on "light" mysticism in Islam generally, Franz Rosenthal, *Knowledge Triumphant* (Leiden, 1970), ch. 6.

[8] See A. Jeffrey, *Materials for the History of the Text of the Qur'ān* (Leiden, 1937), pp. 65, 149.

[9] On the meaning of such terms, see Wolfson, "Amphibolous Terms" (cited in n.3 above).

[10] "On the Proof of Prophecies," tr. Michael E. Marmura in Ralph Lerner and Muhsin Mahdi, eds., *Medieval Political Philosophy* (Ithaca, N.Y., 1972), p. 116.

[11] Pages 202-3, cited by Soheil Afnan, *Avicenna, His Life and Works* (London, 1958), pp. 192-93.

[12] **Guide**, pp. 6-7.

[13] *Ibid.*, p. 8.

[14] *Ibid.*, pp. 42-43.

[15] *Ibid.*, p. 71. For statements representing the danger of esoteric knowledge in Greek and Muslim writers, see the examples given by George Hourani in the excellent notes to his translation of Ibn Rushd, *Averroes On the Harmony of Religion and Philosophy* (London, 1961), pp. 106-7, n.142.

[16] **Guide**, pp. 81, 111; cf. *Averroes On the Harmony of Religion*, p. 60 and n.138, and p. 65.

[17] Metaphysics 10.2; tr. Michael E. Marmura in Lerner and Mahdi, *Medieval Political Philosophy* p. 100.

[18] Fragment 10, Rose; translated Frederick C. Grant, *Hellenistic Religions* (N.Y., 1953), pp. 73-74.

[19] Richard Walzer, "Al-Farabi's Theory of Prophecy and Divination," *Journal of Hellenic Studies* 77 (1957): 142-48.

[20] **Guide**, p. 280.

[21] Tr. Fauzi M. Najjar in Lerner and Mahdi, *Medieval Political Philosophy*, p. 35.

[22] **Guide**, p. 374.

[23] Afnan, *Avicenna*, p. 179.

[24] **Guide**, p. 375.

[25] *Kuzari* V. 12; cf. on this Wolfson, "The Internal Senses in Latin, Arabic and Hebrew Philosophic Texts, *Harvard Theological Review* 38 (1935) 95-97, 104-05.

[26] **Mishneh Torah,** ***Mada^c, "Yesodey ha-Torah"*** 7.6.

[27] **Guide**, p. 378.

[28] *Op. cit.*, tr. in *Medieval Political Philosophy*, p. 36; cf. also E.I.J. Rosenthal, *Political Thought in Medieval Islam* (Cambridge, 1968), p. 128.

[29] **Guide**, p. 126.

[30] *Nic. Ethics* I.7, 1097 b 11; cf. my "Attaining 'Happiness' (*Eudaimonia*) in Medieval Muslim and Jewish Philosophy," *Centerpoint* 4 (1981): 21-32.

[31] *Meditations* V. xvi.

[32] Cf. Even Shmuel's edition of **Moreh nevukhim**, notes to I. 50, and ch. 2 of **The Eight Chapters of Maimonides on Ethics**, ed. and tr. Joseph I. Gorfinkle (N.Y., 1912).

[33] **Guide**, pp. 111, 619.

[34] **Guide**, p. 619.

[35] *Alfarabi's Philosophy of Plato and Aristotle*, tr. Muhsin Mahdi (revised paper edition, Ithaca, N.Y., 1969), p. 13.

[36] *Al-Fārābī's Short Commentary on Aristotle's Prior Analytics*, tr. Nicholas Rescher (Pittsburgh, 1963), p. 123.

[37] Translated in *Medieval Political Philosophy*, pp. 39-41.

[38] **Guide**, p. 117, and cf. p. 247.

[39] Cf. generally Afnan, *Avicenna*, p. 115 ff., and especially p. 125.

[40] **Guide**, p. 163.

[41] **Mishneh Torah,** *Mada^c, "Yesodey ha-Torah"* 2.10 (and cf. also 2.9). My translation follows in the text.

[42] *Enneads* III.8 (tr. Stephen MacKenna [London, 1969], p. 245).

[43] Franz Rosenthal, *Knowledge Triumphant* (Leiden, 1970), p. 188. See also al-Fārābī's *al-Madīnah al-faḍilah* (cf. Majid Fakhry, *History of Muslim Philosophy* [N.Y., 1970], p. 136), and Ibn Rushd (Averroes), *Tahafut al-tahafut*, tr. Simon Van den Bergh (London, 1954), p. 181, lines 8-10.

[44] *Al-Ibanah ^{c}an-uṣul ad-diyānah*, tr. Walter Klein (New Haven, 1940), p. 88, and cf. p. 95.

[45] **Guide**, p. 170.

[46] Cf. Aristotle, *De Anima* 2. 413 b 23; *Rhetoric* 4. 1381 a 7.

[47] *Tahafut al-tahafut*, tr. van den Bergh, p. 88.

[48] *Ibid.*, p. 90; see the important, spurious, quotation there from "Aristotle" on creation and will (cf. the notes in vol. 2), and cf. **Guide**, p. 297.

[49] "Possibility of the Universe in Al-Farabi, Ibn Sina and Maimonides, (see n. 3 above), p. 45, n. 15.

Maimonides on Hebrew Language and Poetry

This year (1985) marks the 850th anniversary of the birth of Moses b. Maimon (more correctly, Maymūn), known to the world as "Maimonides." He stands, without question, at the pinnacle of Jewish scholarship in all things, a veritable Moses atop the mountain, from whose "overflow" (to use his own philosophical term) knowledge of law, the Mishnah, logic, philosophy and metaphysics, medicine, comparative religion, biblical interpretation, and a host of other things poured forth to the masses below. Even today, nearly a millenium later, almost no one doubts his supreme authority and the ancient motto, already coined in his lifetime, still stands: "From Moses unto Moses, none arose like Moses."[1]

While there has been some work done on the nature of Hebrew translation in the medieval period, the question of attitudes toward Hebrew and the nature of languge in general still needs further investigation.[2] Maimonides himself was a linguist of no small accomplishment, and in addition to the references to be found scattered throughout all of his writings, we need to be reminded that he himself composed a dictionary of medical drugs in Arabic, Greek, Persian, Berber and Spanish.[3] The extent of his knowledge of languages has not, as far as I am aware, been investigated at all.

It is well known that throughout the **Guide**, and particularly in the first part of it, Maimonides deals frequently with biblical words and expressions and their specific meanings. Indeed, under the somewhat misleading title of "biblical exegesis" of Maimonides (for, in fact, he never commented on the Bible as such) this has been the subject of works by Bacher and others.

Maimonides was aware that, still in his day, the scientific study of the Hebrew language and its grammar was not complete. Thus he makes the statement: "we know that today we have no complete understanding of the science of our language and that in all languages rules merely conform to the majority of cases."[4]

Maimonides was well aware of the work of his predecessors in Spain to formulate a scientific explanation of the Hebrew language. Unquestionably the greatest of these was Abu'l-Walīd Marwān (Jonah) Ibn Janāḥ (b. ca. 985-990).[5] Apparently the indebtedness of Maimonides to Ibn Janāḥ has not been hitherto realized, but the fact is that virtually every grammatical and etymological statement made in the **Guide** comes directly, usually without acknowledgement, from the work of the great grammarian. Examples include the explanation of the verb *yalad* (**Guide** I.7, p.32; cf. Ibn Janāḥ, *Shorashim*, s.v. *"y-l-d"*),[6] the meaning of *adam* (**Guide** I.14, p. 40; the examples are all from *Shorashim*, s.v. "*a-d-m*"), the entire discussion of the different meanings of "*lev*" (heart) is based almost verbatim on Ibn Janāḥ (**Guide** I. 39, p. 88; *Shorashim*, s.v. "*l-b-b*"), in one place only, he cites Ibn Janāḥ explicitly (**Guide** I. 43, p. 93), but on the preceding page he also says that "many instances of this use [of "in"] have been enumerated by the linguists" (**Guide** I. 41, p. 92), and he means Ibn Janāḥ, in another of his works.[7] That same work is the source, verbatim, for his statement: "the Hebrew language substitutes the apprehension made by one sense for that made by another," and for the examples he gives.[8]

The Mishnah itself contains few explicit references to the Hebrew language.[9] Thus, we do not find in Maimonides' commentary on the text of the Mishnah anything relating to our subject. Only one point is of interest, and it is a technicality. The Mishnah explains (*Soṭah* 8.1) that the priest "anointed for war"—i.e., who must exhort the soldiers to prepare for battle and exempt those who are mentioned in the Bible (Deuteronomy 20.2ff.)—must speak "in the holy language." In his **Sefer ha-miṣvot** ("Book of commandments"), Positive Commandment No. 191, Maimonides describes in detail what the anointed priest does but he fails to mention that he must announce all this in Hebrew specifically. Yet in **Mishneh Torah** (Code of law), ***Shofṭim: Melakhim*** 7.3, he does say "and he says to them in the holy language..." The explanation for this apparent discrepancy is, I think, simple. The "Book of commandments" deals only with the basic biblical commandment, and the laws in connection with these are only those which are unquestionably biblical; whereas in the "Code," Maimonides includes also those laws which are from the rabbis. The obligation to recite in the Hebrew language must be considered rabbinical, even though derived from analogy from biblical sources.

Maimonides, as indicated already, was himself something of an accomplished linguist. He was born and grew up in Córdoba in Muslim Spain. Like all Jews of that land, his native tongue was thus Arabic. He was extremely proficient in this language (contrary to the views of some nineteenth-century scholars who constantly criticized what they felt to be errors in his Arabic style, without considering what was standard style in Muslim Spain of that time). He himself tells us that he studied with great Muslim scholars, and of course he read all the standard works in Arabic on logic, mathematics, science, medicine, and philosophy.

Almost all of his work, from his first known composition written when he was a teenager and still in Spain (the treatise on logic), and including his commentary on the Mishnah, his medical works, many of his responsa, and the **Guide**, were written in Arabic. Only one work, the **Mishneh Torah**, his monumental code covering all of the laws recorded in both Talmuds and extending over fourteen volumes of text, was composed in Hebrew. As he himself says in his introduction to that work, he desired to compose it in "clear language" so that it would be understood by all. This, indeed, he accomplished with admirable success. The style of the Hebrew in **Mishneh Torah** is so perfect and so simple that it may easily be understood by most readers of Hebrew; something which certainly cannot be claimed for other medieval Hebrew compositions. It would be no exaggeration to say that the style of this work, in fact, is the most perfect ever achieved in the Hebrew language.[10]

In his introduction to **Sefer ha-miṣvot**, he explains that he decided not to compose the **Mishneh Torah** in the Hebrew of the Bible, for that holy language "is too limited for us today to complete in it all the matters relating to the laws," nor in the language of the Talmud, for it is not widely understood, but rather in the language of the Mishnah so that it would be easy to understand for the majority of the people.

Yet for all of Maimonides' proficiency with Arabic, he did not apparently share the veneration for that language which was typical of some of the Jewish writers of the age. In his extremely important letter to Samuel b. Judah Ibn Tibbon (born in Granada, but lived in Provence), who translated Maimonides' work into Hebrew for those who did not understand Arabic, Maimonides praised him for his knowledge of Arabic but observed that it was only a branch of Hebrew: "And I have been amazed how the nature of a son born among the 'stammerers' [*ᶜillgim*, those who don't speak Arabic] can be thus, that he pursues wisdom and is so fluent in the Arabic language, which is certainly Hebrew that has been changed a little."[11] (Apparently Maimonides did not yet know, as he later learned, that Samuel was in fact born in Granada.

In one of his medical works, he cites Galen,[12] who said that Greek is the most pleasant (*ᶜidhab*) of languages, and that this is due to the climate in which the Greeks live. All of this Maimonides says he agrees with, but adds that Galen did not mean just the Greek language, but also the languages of the Arabs, Hebrews, Syrians, and Persians, all of whom share this climate.[13]

This is particularly interesting in light of what he says in **Mishneh Torah, "Tefillah"** 1.4:

> Because Israel was exiled in the days of Nebuchadnezzar the wicked, they became intermingled with Persia and Greece and the other peoples and gave birth to children in the lands of the Gentiles, and the language of these children became corrupted and the language of each individual was compounded of many languages [i.e., influenced by the different languages of the countries where they lived].

His ultimate point there is that for these reasons the rabbis had to ordain a particular order and text of prayers for everyone to recite.

In his somewhat suspect letter (at least part of the

introduction must be a forgery) to Joseph Ibn Jābir ("bonesetter" in Arabic) of Baghdad, his correspondent has complained to him that he did not understand the **Mishneh Torah** because it was in Hebrew! Maimonides first assures him that he is not ignorant (*ᶜam ha-areṣ*), since the important thing is to understand the law, "and there is no difference whether you understand it in the holy language or in Arabic or Aramaic, the intent is the understanding of the matters in whatever language; and certainly [this is so] with regard to commentaries and compositions." Nevertheless, he adominishes him: "It is desirable for you also to learn this lesson from the composition [**M.T.**] in the holy language in which we composed it, for it is easy to understand and accessible to learn. And after you have become instructed in one book you will understand all of the composition in its entirety. But I do not want in any circumstance to bring it out in the Arabic language, for all its style would be lost; and I desire now to return the commentary on the Mishnah and the **Sefer ha-miṣvot** to the holy language, and certainly [not] to return this composition to Arabic, and do not ask this of me at all."[14]

Similarly, in his well-known responsum to the community of Tyre, Maimonides says concerning the **Sefer ha-miṣvot**: "I have greatly regretted that I wrote it in Arabic, because everyone needs to read it, and I wait now that I can translate it into the holy language, with the help of the Almighty."[15] This was not to be, but the work nevertheless was finally translated into Hebrew three different times in the medieval period.

Finally, there is another aspect of languge in the work of Maimonides which is of interest. His doctrine of the "golden mean" is well known, of course. One should avoid excesses and extremes in all things, and he generally followed the traditional Jewish abhorrence of extreme asceticism. However, this was in his writings for the "masses," but as a philosopher he urged the most extreme asceticism and total denial of physical pleasures.[16]

In his commentary on **Avot** ("Ethics of the fathers") Maimonides distinguishes five categories of speech. These are prescribed, prohibited, rejected, desired, and permitted. As an example of the fourth category, desired, he gives "to bestir the soul to virtues through prose and poetry" (*al-khūṭab wa'l-sh-ᶜar*).[17]

He concludes his discussion of poetry by saying that it is not the language but the content which makes a poem objectionable or not; however, were one of the poems Hebrew and the other Arabic, or some other language, listening to the Hebrew poem would be more objectionable since this exalted language should only be used for noble purposes.

In the introduction to **Sanhedrin** 10 ("*Ḥeleq*") Maimonides warns against reading certain books which are a mere waste of time (such as Ben Sira, historical chronicles, and the like), and then appears a phrase which some have translated as "books of songs" (*sifrey ha-niggun*) and others as "books of poetry" (*sifrey ha-shirim*).[18] However, the Arabic is *kutub al-aghānī*, which unequivocably means "books of song," and not poetry. Thus, his objection to these is not that they are of prohibited content, but merely a waste of time.

Similarly, his well-known responsum dealing with music (incidentally, the Arabic text of the question uses the very same word for "song" as the above) elicits from him the reply that it is prohibited to listen to music at all, with or without words, and he cites his above-mentioned commentary on **Avot** where he stated there was no difference in this between Arabic and Hebrew words, but the prohibition depends on the subject. "In truth," he concludes, "it is prohibited to hear a foolish thing even if said not in verse."[19]

Furthermore, to return to Maimonides' commentary on **Avot**, he adds that if the theme of both the theoretical *muwashshahāt* was the same, to arouse lust, it is vice and in the category of rejected speech; however, were one of the poems Hebrew and the other Arabic or Romance, listening to the one in Hebrew would be more objectionable. And if verses from the Torah or from Song of Songs were to be included in the Hebrew *muwashshaḥ*, this would automatically cause it to come under the category not of merely rejected but of prohibited speech.

"For the Torah prohibits making prophetic language types of song of depravity and vileness.

Now these statements of Maimonides have been commented upon more than once. Neal Kozody offers the most recent discussion, in an article not without merit in spite of the author's inability to consult the original Arabic text.[20] Yet Kozody arrived at several false conclusions, such as that the kind of wine banquet to which Maimonides refers must have been some kind of religious ceremony and this explains the objection to the poetry. This, however, is not so, for wine banquets (actually all-night parties in which drinking of wine was accompanied by dancing boys and girls and the beautiful boy who was the cupbearer was the object of much amorous attention) were a common event in the lives of both Muslims and Jews in medieval Spain. What Maimonides is describing is something which he, as a young man in Córdoba, probably witnessed often, and certainly had heard about.

Nor is it, of course, true that the love poems to which Maimonides objects, however much "wonderment" or "dismay" they may cause the author, may actually be allegorical and referring to God. I have already dealt with this subject at length elsewhere.[21]

What is most significant here, and a fact which has gone unremarked by some who have dealt with this section of the commentary (since they rely entirely either on faulty Hebrew translations or faulty English translations) is that Maimonides specifically and repeatedly refers not just to *poems*, but to *muwashshaḥāt*.[22] It is, in fact, true that most of the Hebrew types of this poem which we have deal precisely with the matters to which Maimonides objects: love, usually of boys, dealt with in terms of lust, and the frequent use of biblical terms and allusions.

Maimonides, in fact, was not completely opposed to poetry in general. In fact, he himself composed some poetry.[23] In one of his letters, he even cites a line from a poem by Judah ha-Levy.[24] The objection is not to the *form*, but to the *matter*: the content.

That this is the correct interpretation of Maimonides'

position is demonstrated conclusively from a source which has never been considered in the discussion of the problem, **Guide** III.8 (p. 435). There he calls attention to the severity of the prohibition against obscene language. Speech is one of the peculiar benefits of man, and "should not be used with a view to the greatest deficiency and utter disgrace, so that one says what the ignorant and sinful Gentiles say in their songs and their stories." (Again, the translation is not totally correct, for the Arabic text has not "songs and stories" but poetry [*ashᶜar*] and chronicles [*akhbār*].) Whoever recites poetry about such things as drinking or copulation has committed an act of disobedience to God, no less. Finally, he concludes:

> I can also give the reason why this our language is called the Holy Language...For in this Holy Language no word at all has been laid down in order to designate either the male or the female organ of copulation, nor are there words designating the act itself that brings about generation, the sperm, the urine or the excrements.

This, then, is the reason why Maimonides objects—not to *all* poetry, but to love poetry, for it arouses lust and vile desires and defiles the holy language.

How little has been understood the actual attitude of Maimonides with regard to poetry is evident from the claim of Isadore Twersky, that poetry "aroused Maimonides' ire" and that he "indiscriminately lambasted their authors." Further, he says, "with a mixture of Platonic disdain and Voltairean irony, Maimonides, who had little use for poetry of any kind, even liturgical and hymnal, dismissed these writers as 'poets, not scholars.'"[25] Let us see whether what Maimonides actually said warrants such rhetoric.

In the source which Twersky rather too broadly cites, **Guide** I.59 (actually only p. 141), Maimonides criticizes the "truly ignorant" who spoke at great length in prayers and sermons they composed, predicating attributes of God which are not suitable. "This kind of license," he concludes, "is frequently taken by poets and preachers or such as think that what they speak is poetry, so that the utterances of some of them constitute an absolute denial of faith, while other utterances contain such rubbish and such perverse imaginings as to make men laugh when they hear them..." Maimonides, again, is not opposed to poems and poets of every kind, but only (in this case) those kinds of religious poems which attribute to God undesirable or incorrect attributes.

Maimonides was asked, more than once, his opinion about the propriety of reciting *piyyuṭim* (liturgical poems) in the service. He steadfastly maintained, not that this was forbidden, but that they must not be recited in such a manner as to interrupt the text of the blessings in the prayers as instructed by the rabbis.[26] In one of these responsa, to be sure, he criticizes *piyyuṭim* as adding words and matters which are not of the nature or subject of the prayer, "and there are added to this meters and melodies, and prayer goes out of the boundaries of prayer and is made a matter of laughter." This also causes people to talk in the middle of the service, sensing that these are not real prayer. "In addition to this, these *piyyuṭim* are *sometimes* [my emphasis] the words of poets, not scholars," which causes people to think they should use these words and not the words of the prophets for prayer.[27]

Similar language is used by Maimonides in his introduction to **Sefer ha-miṣvot** (alluded to by Twersky):

> And so every time that I heard the *Azharot* [*piyyuṭim* enumerating the commandments] so many in number which were composed by those among us in Spain, 'my pains are come upon me' [Daniel 10.16] because of what I have seen of the popularity and widespread nature of these; and *even though they are not to be blamed* [my emphasis], since their composers are *payyeṭanim* and not rabbis...

and indeed they have composed the poems in faith, but his objection is that they have followed one of the works of an earlier rabbi in enumerating the commandments, and Maimonides disagrees with that enumeration.[28]

Obviously, it is completely incorrect to distort these statements, which refer to specific objections against specific types of poems, into the sweeping generalization which Twersky has set forth in a book for the public not able, for the most part, to read the original (Arabic) sources! Still wider from the truth is the distortion that Maimonides "dismissed" all poets as "poets, not scholars." What he said, in fact, is that *some* liturgical poems were composed by poets, not scholars; and his intent was not to "dismiss" the poets, but to caution against accepting these kinds of poems instead of prayer. In the source on which Twersky relied, indeed, his intention was not to "dismiss" them at all, but to say that even though he finds the enumeration of the commandments in this particular kind of poem objectionable, the authors are certainly *not* to be blamed, for they are poets, not rabbis.

Finally, we should note that in spite of the fact that he objected in an earlier responsum to the recitation of some *piyyuṭim* composed by Saᶜadyah Gaon, only because they interrupt the prayers, he later retracted and says these are "very lovely and desirable in order to arouse the intention" in prayer, but still it should not be done in the synagogue, but rather before the public prayers.[29]

Notes

[1] One would imagine that no one today would criticize Maimonides, least of all in his more "orthodox" writings; yet this is not the case, as witness the recent article by Haym Soloveitchik "Maimondes' '*Iggeret Ha-Shemad*: Law and Rhetoric," in *Sefer zikharon le-ha-rav Yosef Ḥayyim Lukstiin* (Rabbi Joseph H. Lookstein Memorial Volume) (N.Y., 1980), pp. 281-319. The attack on Maimonides there is not worthy of a scholar of Soloveitchik's standing.

The phrase "*mi-Mosheh le-Mosheh lo' qam ke-Mosheh*" was already used by Judah al-Ḥarizi in the introduction to his translation of Maimonides' commentary on the Mishnah.

[2] See, e.g., H. Hirschfeld, *Literary History of Hebrew Grammarians and Lexicographers* (Oxford, 1926); A.S. Halkin, "The Medieval Jewish Attitude toward Hebrew," in Alexander Altmann, ed., *Biblical and Other Studies* (Cambridge, Mass., 1963), pp. 233-48 (still almost the only article on the subject, but it is marred by numerous errors of fact and interpretation); E.Y. Kutscher, *A History of the Hebrew Language* (Leiden, 1982), p. 158ff.; Roth, "Jewish Reactions to *ᶜArabiyya* and the Renaissance of Hebrew in Spain," *Journal of Semitic Studies* 28 (1983): 63-84. I plan a future study on medieval Jewish and Muslim theories of language.

[3] See M. Meyerhoff, "Sur un glossaire...," *Bulletin de l'institut d'Egypte* 17 (1934-35): 233-35.

[4] **Guide of the Perplexed**, tr. Shlomo Pines (Chicago, 1963), p.162.

[5] Some important studies include José Manuel Camcho Padilla, "Rabí Yonâ ben Gannach," *Boletín de la real academia de ciencias, bellas letras y nobles artes de Córdoba* 8 (1929): 23-72 (an extremely important article, which also includes the text and translation of a fragment of an unknown work of his); Shraga Abramson, "*ᶜAl sheney sifrey diqduq*," *Leshonenu* 26 (1961): 24-26; and Edna Amir Coffin, "Ibn Janāḥ's Kitāb al-Lumaᶜ: An Integration of Medieval Grammatical Approaches," *Michigan Oriental Studies in honor of George C.*

Cameron (Ann Arbor, 1976), pp. 65-79; an important article which merits wider dissemination.

[6] Ibn Janāḥ, *Sefer ha-shorashim*, ed. W.Z. Bacher (Berlin, 1896; photo rpt. Amsterdam, 1969). As I have written elsewhere, this is the single most important medieval Hebrew dictionary.

[7] *Sefer ha-riqmah* (K. al-lumaᶜ), ed. M. Wilensky (Berlin, 1929; photo rpt., Jerusalem, 1964), "*Shaᶜar*" 6 (vol. I, 83ff.).

[8] *Ibid.*, "*Shaᶜar*" 28 (vol. I, 320, line 14ff.).

[9] *Yevamot* 12.6; *Soṭah* 7.2 - 4; 8.1; 9.1; *Yadayim* 4.5.

[10] See on Maimonides' style in *M.T.* Kutscher, *op. cit.*,pp.165-66.

[11] Moses b. Maimon, **Qoveṣ teshuvot** (Leipzig, 1859; photo rpt. Gregg International Publishers [England], 1969) II, 27c.

[12] For the identification of this work by Galen, see S. Muntner, "*Zihuy sifrey Galinus ha-nizkarim ᶜal-yedey ha-Rambam be-sifro 'Pirqey Mosheh',*" *ha-Rofe ha-ᶜIvri* 27 (1954): 4, note 5.

[13] Fragment of **Pirqey Mosheh**, ed. and tr. Joseph Kafiḥ in his edition of Moses b. Maimon, **Iggrot** (Jerusalem, 1972), pp. 148-50 (apparently overlooked by Kafiḥ, the text already appeared in **Qoveṣ teshuvot** II, 22d-23a). See also the very similar discussion of this in Moses Ibn Ezra, *Kitāb al-muḥādara wa'l-mudhākara*, ed. and tr. A.S. Halkin (Jerusalem, 1975), p. 41 and pp. 31 and 33.

[14] **Qoveṣ** II, 15.

[15] Moses b. Maimon, **Teshuvot**, ed. Joshua Blau (Jerusalem, 1960), II. 725.

[16] It hardly seems necessary to prove this obvious point. See, for example, **Guide** I.5 (p. 30), 35 (p. 79), II.23 (p. 321), 36 (p. 371), III.8 (pp. 432-34), 12 (pp. 445-46), 33 (p. 532). Nor is it only in his philosophical work that Maimonides takes an extreme position; his other more "popular" writings are almost equally severe.

[17] Commentary on *Avot*, ed. (Arabic) and tr. (Hebrew) E. Baneth in *Jubelschrift zum...Israel Hildesheimer* (Berlin, 1890), p. 71.

[18] Texts: **Haqdamot le-feirush ha-mishnah**, ed. Mordecai

Rabinowitz (Jerusalem, 1961), p. 135; **Mishnah ᶜim peirush rabbeinu Mosheh ben Maimon**, ed. Joseph Kafiḥ (Jerusalem, 1965) IV (**Neziqin**), p. 141. See my translation, above, p. 50

[19] **Teshuvot**, ed. Blau, II. 398-99.

[20] "Reading Medieval Hebrew Love Poetry," *Association for Jewish Studies (AJS) Review* 2 (1977): 111-29 (to be fair to Kozodoy, I had not yet begun to publish the results of my own research on this type of poetry when this was written).

[21] Particularly in "'Deal Gently with the Young Man': Love of Boys in Medieval Hebrew Poetry of Spain," *Speculum* 57 (1982): 20-51. References to other work may be found there. On real allegorical use of love imagery, see my article "My Beloved is Like a Gazelle: Imagery of the Beloved Boy in Religious Hebrew Poetry," *Hebrew Annual Review* 9 (1985).

[22] Only Ḥayyim Schirmann was aware of this, and in his *Shirim ḥadashim min ha-genizah* (Jerusalem, 1965), p. 297, quotes this comment of Maimonides and connects it with *muwashshaḥāt* poetry. However, he surmised that the responsum dealing with music which we have cited may be connected with Maimonides' objection to poetry, which was probably sung. But there is no evidence to support the theory that poetry was sung, nor did Maimonides object to poetry *per se*, as Schirmann himself had already observed in an earlier article, "*ha-Rambam ve-ha-shirah ha-ᶜivrit*," *Moznayim* 3 (1935): 433-36.

[23] See Schirmann's article, *ibid.*, p. 434; M. Steinschneider, "*Moreh maqom ha-moreh*," *Qoveṣ ᶜal-yad* I (1885) and II (1886); W. Bacher, "Hebräische verse von Maimuni," *M.G.W.J.* 53 (1909): 581-88; A. Marx in *J.Q.R.* (n.s.) 25 (1935): 383 (dubious) and 389 (authentic).

[24] **Qoveṣ teshuvot** II. 27b; Judah ha-Levy, *Divan*, ed. H. Brody, I, 124.

[25] *Introduction to the Code of Maimonides* (New Haven, 1980), p. 250 and n. 29. (See my critical review of this book in *Hebrew Studies* 24 [1983]: 226-29, and below in this volume.)

[26] *Teshuvot*, ed. Blau, II. 328, 363-66, 366-70, 465-68, 486, 489, 490-91.

[27] *Ibid.*, pp. 467-68.

[28] **Sefer ha-miṣvot**, tr. Joseph Kafiḥ (Jerusalem, 1958), p. 4.

[29] **Teshuvot**, II, 490-91.

[30] Here, too, he was following models in Muslim philosophy. On the question of the "attainment of happiness," see my "Attaining 'Happiness' (*Eudaimonia*) in Medieval Muslim and Jewish Philosophy," *Centerpoint* 4 (1981): 21-32.

Introduction to the Code of Maimonides (*Mishneh Torah*)

by Isadore Twersky (New Haven, 1980)
Critical Review-Essay

(Revised version of review which appeared in *Hebrew Studies* 24 (1983): 226-29.)

The **Mishneh Torah** of Maimonides remains the only complete code of Jewish law by virtue of its attempt to codify all the laws of the Talmud, whether currently applicable or not (many of the talmudic laws, and biblical laws upon which they are based, are restricted by time, place or circumstance, some applicable only in the Land of Israel, others only in the Temple, or at the time when the Temple was standing).

The Yale University Press has for some years been issuing, slowly and laboriously and in uneven quality, English translations of these volumes. The question has to be asked for whom these volumes are intended, since there is little evidence that Jewish scholars ever look at them, and no evidence that non-Jewish scholars do. Nevertheless, the present introductory volume deserves to be read (or more correctly, consulted) by any student of Jewish religion and law. It must be said, however, that the book is not without its problems.

One of the problems is the scope of the book. An introduction should be just that: a brief and readable guide to the use of that which it seeks to introduce, with some analysis of historical background and the nature of the work, and perhaps of its influence on subsequent works of a similar nature. Twersky's book seems to be more of an excuse for the author to provide us with everything he knows about Maimonides (and a good deal of other things as well). It is long and difficult, at times even tedious, and does not lend itself to easy use or consultation by the "general reader" (!) for whom it is claimed to have been written (in fact, the careful reader of this tome will have to be a rather thoroughly trained scholar of Jewish sources). It is not until the Epilogue that some of the points suggested above are even touched upon, in truly an afterthought manner (possibly the result of editorial suggestion). At the end of the book is a list of the Hebrew titles of the various treatises of the Code, but not the English titles actually used in the Yale series, nor a subject listing with reference to volume and page. The reader with the patience to finish this book will still have only the vaguest idea as to what the Code is about.

Since there is no discussion by Twersky of anything so mundane as when the Code was composed, let us begin by stating that Maimonides himself provides us some interesting information in a very important letter to Jonathan ha-Kohen of Lunel (who corresponded with Maimonides concerning some questions which the Provençal rabbis had on the Code). After referring to his being ill for about a year, and the great "troubles" which befell him, he goes on to say:

> I lie most of the day on my bed, and the yoke of the Gentiles is upon my neck in matters of medicine which sap my strength, for they do not leave me a single hour day and night—and what can I do since my nature [reputation] is known in the majority of the lands? Furthermore, I am not today like I was in my youth, but my strength is feeble...

He concludes by stating tht he had worked some ten years in composing the Code. Solomon Gandz has argued fairly convincingly that it was completed in its final version in 1178, and thus the ten year period to which Maimonides here refers must have been approximately 1168-1178.[1]

We are still in desperate need of a thorough scholarly analysis of the extant manuscripts, including the various holograph manuscripts and fragments.[2]

Such an analysis should consider the language used by the author, revisions made, and his general methodology of composition (Kafiḥ made a few such observations in his introduction to his Hebrew translation of Maimonides' Commentary on the Mishnah). Twersky's few remarks on this are wholly inadequate.

Minor problems abound in Twersky's book. Names are often misspelled—e.g., Ibn Megas (Ibn Megash), Judah Albargeloni (a long outdated form, for Judah b. Barzilay al-Barṣiloniy), Ibn Gikatilia (!), Joseph Jabez, etc. References are not always correct; e.g., p. 58, n. 93: of three references to the supposed Maimonidean **Treatise on Resurrection** (actually most likely a forgery), only one (p. 21) is relevant; none of the talmudic references in the note is correct. There are frequent errors in page citations of Kafiḥ's edition of the commentary on the Mishnah. The term *dīwān* is used several times to describe the Code, with the Arabic term rendered in the sense of "collection." The term, probably derived from Persian, was, it is true, used in the early Islamic period to mean a treasury account or register. Later, long before Maimonides, and continuing throughout the medieval period, it came to mean a book of poetry (only), or a bureau of government. It never had the meaning of "book" or "composition."[3] In his Arabic letters, Maimonides refers to the Code as *al-ḥibur* or *al-talif*, and if Twersky felt constrained to find an Arabic term to apply to a work written entirely in Hebrew (why?), he might have consulted someone who reads Arabic to find what terms Maimonides himself used.

More serious errors of fact and of interpretation are also present, which can only mislead and confuse the "general reader" for whom the book was written. We read with astonishment that Spanish Jews only knew three orders of the Talmud! (p. 8). Since no substantiation is offered for this statement, it can perhaps be assumed that the author was misled by a statement of Kafiḥ, who says that only the orders of *Mo*ᶜ*ed* and *Nezikin* ("Festivals" and "Damages") were found in a complete state among the Jews of Yemen.[4] Yemen, however, is not Spain, and one can only wonder as to what caused Twersky to arrive at his peculiar conclusion. Any "student of a rabbinical school," to use the familiar expression, knows very well that

Spanish Jewish scholars not only utilized but commented upon the entire Talmud (not to mention that Maimonides himself composed, or started to compose, such a commentary).

One must admire the author for his wide reading in fields that have little or nothing to do with the subject at hand, but in some cases this appears to have resulted in other errors, such as the statement (p. 60) that the problem of the nature of law was totally irrelevant to medieval scholars (not just to *Jewish* scholars, but *all* medieval scholars, presumably). Such a statement is not only totally erroneous, it is embarrassing to those who work on medieval subjects. Both medieval Muslim and Christian scholars, as well as Jewish, exhibited considerable interest in the nature of law, and it was of course not irrelevant to Maimonides, who has in fact much to say on this subject. Not only in the **Mishneh Torah**, but in his other writings and particularly in the **Guide**, there is discussion bearing on this subject (it is unfortunate, indeed, that Pines in his translation of the latter work throughout translates "Law"—with a capital L—for any term referring to law, divine or secular, Jewish or general, thus making it impossible to determine what Maimonides is discussing without having recourse to the original Arabic).[5] We are in need of a complete analysis of Maimonides' views on the nature of law, in fact.

The discussion of the messianic views of Maimonides (p. 67) is of interest, but it is unfortunate that the author did not refer to Solomon Zeitlin, *Maimonides, a biography* (New York, 1935), chapter eight. Zeitlin argued that the **Mishneh Torah** was in part a model "constitution" for a restored Jewish state which he fervently expected; a view which certainly is not without merit.[6]

While it certainly is not fair to expect a non-Islamicist to have extensive knowledge of Muslim sources, nevertheless a considerable amount of work has been done in English on these subjects. Thus, one of the major disappointments of Twersky's book is its failure to give careful consideration to the probability (almost certainty) of Muslim influences on Maimonides' codification (see, e.g., pp. 77, 110, 258). The "Book of Knowledge" is discussed at some length, but Franz Rosenthal's vitally important *Knowledge Triumphant, the concept of knowledge in medieval Islam* is only casually cited in a footnote, and was not apparently read carefully. It is, therefore, perhaps appropriate here to note again that Rosenthal (pp. 95-96) explains that the puzzling fact that Maimonides opened his Code (intended, after all, for the masses) with the deeply metaphysical "Book of Knowledge" must be understood in light of a long Muslim tradition of such books, particularly in Muslim codes (some of these, such as al-Bukharī's, are available in English translation). Among these, he specifically mentions al-Ghazālī's *Iḥyā'* (also in translation). Yet in spite of these important observations, almost no scholar has paid attention to Rosenthal's suggestion to analyze the relationship between these authorities and Maimonides.[7]

There is much discussion, as there should be, of Maimonides' relation to his famous predecessor Isaac al-Fāsī; but much less adequate treatment is given to his relation to previous geonic compilations, particularly to the work of Sa^cadyah Gaon, but also that of Hai (or Hayya) Gaon and others.

Of interest is the chapter on "Language and Style," which is in some respects the best chapter in the book (see my essay on "Maimonides on Hebrew Language and Poetry" in this volume). In Hebrew prose writing, two giants emerge as models of beauty and clarity of style: Maimonides and "Aḥad ha-^cAm" (Asher Ginzberg, 1856-1927).[8] The student who wishes to know Hebrew correctly must virtually commit to memory the style of these masters. It is thus appropriate that a lengthy chapter be devoted to Maimonides' theories of language and to stylistic elements in the Code (it is, of course, difficult to discuss Hebrew style in a chapter written in English, and perhaps more difficult to justify the inclusion of such a technical subject in a book for the "general reader"). One might wish for more concrete examples of what it is that makes Mamonides the genius he undeniably was in the matter of Hebrew style. Here, again, the question of the influence of predecessors remains unaddressed.

Even this chapter is not without faults which cannot go unremarked. The statement that Hebrew poets of Spain, and particularly Judah ha-Levy, restricted themselves to "pure Biblical Hebrew with no admixture whatsoever of post-Biblical idioms" (p. 332) is totally wrong. Of all the poets to pick to illustrate this erroneous notion, Judah ha-Levy was perhaps the most unfortunate choice.[9] As one who does considerable research in medieval Hebrew poetry, I can state with assurance that this statement is absolutely false. All the classical Hebrew poets of Spain were great innovators in Hebrew language—*most* of all, perhaps, ha-Levy! (Nor is the statement in n. 19 there entirely accurate; Shem Tov Ibn Falquerah, in the place cited, specifically distinguishes between the *classical* ["early"] poets of Spain, whom he rightly calls great innovators, and the later poets of his day whom he says slavishly imitated biblical style. While that judgement must not be accepted uncritically either, it is certainly no support for Twersky's mistaken claim.) This faulty notion was common among scholars of the last century, and one who has little acquaintance with the intricacies of Hebrew poetry should not be faulted for sharing this error; however, caution in making such categorical statements on a subject outside one's range of competence is in order.

The book closes with an extremely lengthy chapter on "Law and Philosophy." There is much erudition here, as throughout the book, but those who have anticipated this long-awaited work as a definitive statement on these and other topics in the **Mishneh Torah** must be somewhat disappointed. There is still room for considerable work to be done.

There is a very extensive bibliography, which we are told is "not a mere alphabetical listing of works cited in the footnotes" (p. 561). Indeed, it is not. Many of the works in the bibliography are not cited in the notes at all, even when they should be. The bibliography, compiled "with the aid" of a rabbi, is padded to the point of being almost useless. Under the heading "Primary Sources," for instance is listed almost every work written by a medieval Jewish writer, and many post-medieval ones. Most of these have nothing to do with Maimonides. Exhaustive as the list is, it is nevertheless not complete. Thus, only a few of the many editions of "*Teshuvot* [responsa] *ha-geonim*" are listed; works by Moses b. Naḥman (Naḥmanides) which have little or nothing to do with Maimonides are listed, but *not* his strictures on Maimonides' "Book of Commandments." English translations of sources are rarely noted (in a book for the "general reader"!). Here, too, names are incorrectly spelled (note "ibn Megas" for "Megash," "Jedaiah Penini" for Yedayah Bedersi, called "ha-Penini," etc.). The total irrelevancy of the "Primary Sources" may be seen in the listing of "Luzzatto, M.H.," an eighteenth-century moralist and dramatist whose work has nothing to do with the Code at all, and "Luzzatto, S."—a source, not for Maimonides, but for the religious practices of Jews of Venice in the seventeenth century! The works of Maimonides, however, are not listed at all.

The long bibliography of "Secondary Literature" is almost as irrelevant, with only some works listed actually pertaining to Maimonides. Better would have been an annotated bibliography, or even a simple listing, of articles and books in languages other than Hebrew which deal specifically with the Code, or at least with legal aspects of Maimonides' work and thought.

The misspelling also of names of renowned modern Jewish scholars ("Aloni" for Alloni, "Ashtour" for Ashtor, "Ibn Shemuel" for Even-Shmuel [Kaufmann], "Maimon, A." for Maimon, Judah Loeb [the same as "Maimon, J."], "Zevin, I." for Zevin, S.J.) does not elicit confidence that all the works listed were, in fact, consulted. It goes without saying that important works have been omitted also in the "Secondary Literature."

There is still a need, then, for an Introduction to the Code **(Mishneh Torah)** of Maimonides; or, perhaps more correctly, two such introductions: one for the general reader who may wish to know what the Code is about, why it was written, and what value it has today, with perhaps some discussion of where in the English translation he can expect to find a discussion of certain topics; the second, a more scholarly volume which will deal with such matters as sources, conception of law, language and style, and the relation of the Code to Maimonides' other writings.

As an aid to the general reader who may meanwhile wish to pursue further this aspect of Maimonides, the following brief bibliography may serve as a guide (most, if not all, the listed works are omitted in Twersky):

1. Various essays in volume one of *Jewish Law Annual* 1978); aside from those mentioned below (note 5), see especially Haim Cohn, “Maimonidean Theories of Codification,” and Nahum Rabinovitch, “Mishneh Torah—Code and Commentary,” which taken together serve as a better introduction than the book under review here.

2. Tchernowitz, Chaim. *Maimonides as Codifier*, Pamphlet III of the Maimonides Octocentennial Series (N.Y., 1935), which could have served as a model for Twersky.

3. Zevin, S.J., “Four Aspects of Maimonides’ Halakhic Genius,” in Aryeh Newman, ed., *Six Talks on Maimonides* (Jerusalem, 1955), pp. 17-21.

4. Goldman, S., “The Halachic Foundation of Maimonides’ Thirteen Principles,” H.J. Zimmels, *et al.*, eds., *Essays presented to Chief Rabbi Israel Brodie...* (London, 1967), pp. 111-18 (a short but insightful article).

5. Benedikt, B.Z. “*Le-darkho shel ha-Rambam bi-fesaq halakhah*,” *Sinai* 50 (1961): 229-38, and “*Le-darkho shel ha-Rambam be-Yad ha-ḥazaqah*,” *ibid.* 52 (1963): 229-86 (though in Hebrew, neither of these important articles is mentioned by Twersky.)

6. Berman, Lawrence V. “Natural Law in Averroes and Maimonides” (May 1, 1979), privately circulated and apparently unpublished; a fine article.

7. Bratton, Fred G. *Maimonides, Medieval Modernist* (Boston, 1967).

8. Faur, José, “*^{c}Iyyunim be-hilkhot teshuvah la-Rambam*,” *Sinai* 61 (1967): 259-66; *idem.* “*Maqor ḥiyyuvan shel miṣvot le-da^{c}at ha-Rambam*,” *Tarbiz* 38 (1969): 43-53.

9. Faur, José. *Meḥqarim ve-^{c}iyyunim be-Mishneh Torah* (Jerusalem, 1978).

10. Laserson, Max M. *ha-Filosofiyah ha-mishpaṭit shel ha-Rambam* (Tel Aviv, 1939): a small, but important, book.

Notes

[1] Moses b. Maimon, **Qoveṣ teshuvot ha-Rambam**, ed. Abraham Lichtenberg (Leipzig, 1859; photo rpt. Gregg International Publishers, Farnborough, England, 1969) I, 12c, No. 49; corrected text in Moses b. Maimon, **Teshuvot ha-Rambam**, ed. Joshua Blau (Jerusalem, 1961) III, pp. 55-57. The date of the letter is difficult to determine; the responsa in reply to the questions were dated 1198 (cf. Blau, p. 43 there), but the letter could have been several years earlier; cf. generally Alexander Marx, "The Correspondence Between the Rabbis of Southern France and Maimonides About Astrology," *Hebrew Union College Annual* 3 (1926): 311-58 (pp. 325-35 are relevant), rpt. in his *Studies in Jewish History and Booklore* (N.Y., 1944), pp. 48-62. Solomon Gandz (not "D. Gandz" as in Twersky), "The Date of the Composition of Maimonides' Code," American Academy for Jewish Research. *Proceedings* 17 (1947): 1-7.

[2] In addition to the sources cited by Marx, *op. cit.*, n. 9, and by Twersky, see S.M. Stern, "Autographs of Maimonides in the Bodleian Library," *Bodleian Library Record* 5 (1955): 180-202; Alexander Scheiber, "Autograph Manuscripts of Maimonides," *Acta Orientalia* (Budapest) 33 (1979): 187-95.

[3] See the word *dīwān* in any standard Arabic dictionary. The entry in the new *Encyclopedia of Islam* is not very helpful, totally ignoring all but the bureaucratic meaning (that it also means a book of poetry, and indeed this is the primary meaning of the word, is not even mentioned!). The term does not appear at all as a title of any extant Judeo-Arabic book in Steinschneider, *Die arabische Literatur der Juden* (Frankfort a.M., 1902); the one reference in the index is an error. Since this review appeared, I have also called attention to another scholar's erroneous discussion of *dīwān* with regard to poetical compilations; see my review of Uriel Simon, "*Four Approaches to the Book of Psalms,*" in *Hebrew Studies* 25 (1984): 212. I hope soon to write an article dealing with the subject in full.

[4] Moses b. Maimon, **Mishnah ᶜim peirush**..., ed. and tr. Joseph Kafiḥ (Jerusalem, 1963) I, 6.

[5] The misconception could be corrected easily by consulting such important articles as Lenn E. Goodman, "Maimonides' Philosophy of Law" (pp. 72-107) and Gerald Blidstein, "Maimonides on Oral Law" (pp. 108-22) in *Jewish Law Annual* 1 (1978). One hardly knows where to begin to correct the misconception concerning medieval interest generally in the nature of law; see, e.g., Gaines Post, *Studies in Medieval Legal Thought* (Princeton, 1969); Thomas Aquinas, *Summa Theologica* 1a-2ae, qu. 90-97; etc.

[6] I have an article in press, "Forgery and Abrogation of the Torah," which deals in part with Maimonides' messianic statements.

[7] Twersky himself cites approvingly H. Lazarus-Yaffeh's article on al-Ghazālī (see p. 363, n. 15)—an article which must nevertheless be used with caution—but says nothing there about Rosenthal. One article which does, however, deal with this, and ought to have been mentioned, is Arthur Hyman, "A Note on Maimonides' Classification of Law," in Salo W. Baron and Isaac Barzilay, eds., *American Academy for Jewish Research Jubilee Volume* (N.Y., 1980) I, 323-43. Lenn Goodman has done some important work on al-Ghazālī, and perhaps he will yet investigate this area.

[8] After this review was published, one reader observed that he agreed completely with my judgement with regard to Maimonides, but not on "Ahad ha-ᶜAm." Most authorities on Hebrew style would, I think, rather be inclined to agree with the analysis; cf., e.g., Tudor Parfitt, "Ahad ha-Am's Role in the Revival and Development of Hebrew," in Jacques Kornberg, ed., *At the Crossroads, Essays on Ahad Ha-am* (Albany, N.Y., 1983), and also David Patterson there, pp. 41-42. In the end, all such statements are perhaps subjective, and the interested reader will perhaps (hopefully) read Ahad ha-ᶜAm's original Hebrew essays.

[9] Almost no work has, in fact, been done on the poets and Hebrew language; see briefly my "Seeing the Bible through a

Poet's Eyes," *Hebrew Studies* 23 (1982): 111-14, and more generally my "Jewish Reactions to the ᶜ*Arabiyya* and the Renaissance of Hebrew in Spain," *Journal of Semitic Studies* 28 (1983): 63-84 (both appeared after Twersky's book, of course).

Maimonides and Spanish Scholarship

Inasmuch as this book is being published under the auspices of the renowned Hispanic Seminary of Medieval Studies, whose works are utilized by scholars of Spanish studies throughout the world, it seems advisable to conclude with a bibliography of books and articles on Maimonides written in the Spanish language, whether by scholars in Spain or elsewhere, and also to note Spanish translations of some of Maimonides' works.

Spain may also be said to lead the world in the area of research on Jewish subjects, ranging from Bible to philology, rabbinic literature, medieval poetry, philosophy, and Jewish history. Almost as soon as the scientific study of Jewish subjects began in the nineteenth century, Spanish scholars were already writing extensively in this field. Often thoroughly trained in Hebrew and Arabic, many of the past and contemporary Christian scholars of Spain have enriched our knowledge with splendid editions and translations of important medieval Hebrew works. The names of Millás Vallicrosa, Gonzàles-Llubera, Cantera Burgos, José Lacava, Alejandro Díez-Macho, David Gonzalo Maeso, Carlos del Valle Rodríguez, and many others will long stand (or should, at any rate) in the annals of Hebrew scholarship. Their work is uniformly careful, thorough and reliable.

Although Maimonides and his family left Spain when he was still young, he had nevertheless written important works while still in Spain, and there he of course received all his training and knowledge. All of his life he considered himself a "Spaniard," and so referred to himself. It is quite fitting, therefore, that he should be claimed by Spain as one of her most important native sons.

Translations of Maimonides in Spanish

(Most of these were done by Jews of Spanish ancestry living

in Amsterdam; the exceptions are only the translations of the **Guide** noted, done by modern scholars.)

1. *Misnajoth con el comento de el* [sic] *Hakam...R. Moseh hijo de Maimon*, tr. Abraham b. Reuben Azulay (Venice, 1606; two vols.). (Commentary on the Mishnah.)

2. *Tratado de los articulos de la Ley Divina*, tr. David de Yshac Cohen de Lara (Amsterdam, 1652; rpt. *Maimonides da Lei Divina*, ed. M. Amzalak [Lisbon, 1925]). Partial translation of introduction to chapter 10 of *Sanhedrin*.

3. *Tratado de la Thesuvah o Contricion*, tr. Semuel de Silva (Amsterdam, 1613), and again as *Tratado de Penitencia*, tr. David Yshac Cohen de Lara (Amsterdam, 1660). Laws of Repentance from *Mishneh Torah*.

4. *Tratado de moralidad y regimenta de la vida*, tr. David Yshac Cohen de Lara (Hamburg, 1662). Medical treatise.

5. Prologues and excerpts of Pedro de Toledo's medieval translation of the *Guide* in Mario Schiff (see below, *Works on Maimonides*, No. 8).

6. Llamas, José. *Maimonides: Siglo XII*. (Madrid, 1936). Contains translations of much of the *Guide*, from the French translation of Munk.

7. *Guía de los descarriados*, tr. (from the French translation of S. Munk) José Suárez Lorenzo with introductions by Ignacio Bauer and Antonio Ballesteros Baretta) (Madrid, 1936). The *Guide*; only Part I.

8. *Guía de los descarriados*, tr. Fernando Valera (Mexico, 1946).

9. *Guía de los descarriados* tr. (from the French) León Dejovne (Buenos Aires, 1955).

10. *Guía de perplejos*, tr. David Gonzalo Maeso (Madrid, 1983). Complete translation, based on Arabic text and Hebrew and English translations, with introduction.

Works on Maimonides in Spanish

1. *Maimónides* (Córdoba, 1935). Centenary volume.

2. Llamás, José. *Maimónides, siglo XII* (Madrid, 1936).

3. Caravacca, Andrés. *Moises ben Maimón* (Madrid, 1903).

4. Bauer y Landauer, Ignacio. *Maimónides, un sabio de la Edad Media* (Madrid, 1935).

5. *Boletín de la Real Academia de las Ciencias de Córdoba* (1950). Entire volume, commemorative.

6. *Maimónides* (N.Y., Instituto de las Españas en Estados Unidos, 1940). Commemorative volume.

7. *Primer simposio de estudios Sefardies* pp. 629-35 (on the erection of the statue of Maimonides in Córdoba).

8. Schiff, Mario, "Una traducción española del 'More Nebuchim.' Notas acerca del manuscrito KK-9 de la Biblioteca Nacional," *Revista Critica de Historia y Literatura Españolas, Portuguesas e Hispano-Americanas* 26 (1897): 160-76, 267. The medieval translation of the *Guide* by Pedro de Toledo; cf. also Mario Schiff, *La Bibliothèque du Marquis de Santillane*, p. 428ff., and Yitzhak Baer in *Tarbiz* 6: 153.

9. Bar-Lewaw, I., "Pedro de Toledo, el primer traductor español del 'More'," *Homenaje a Antonio Rodríguez-Moñino* (Madrid, 1966) I, 57-64; cf. also his "Apuntos sobre la primera traducción española del More Nebujim," *Otsar Yehudei Sefarad* 9 (1966): lxxv-xxxi (in Spanish), and Deborah Rosenblatt, "*Mostrador e enseñador de los turbados*: The First Spanish Translation of Maimonides' **Guide of the Perplexed**," in Izaak Langnas and Barton Sholod, eds., *Studies in Honor of M.J. Benardete* (N.Y., 1965), pp. 47-82.

10. Gonzalo Maeso, David, "Panegírico o corona laudatoria en honor de Maimónides," *Miscelánea de Estudios Arabes y Hebraicos* 12-13 (1963): 295-64

11. Gonzalo Maeso, David. *Manual de Historia de la Literatura Hebrea* (Madrid, 1960), pp. 511-27.

12. Aisenstat, Israel, "Rabí Moises ben Maimon como jurista y como codificador," *Davar* (Buenos Aires) 72 (1957): 63-73.

13. Fuentes Guerra, R. *Ensayos biográficos* (1954).

14. Casciaro, José María. *El diálogo teológico de Santo Tomás con musulmanes y judíos*, (Madrid, 1969).

15. Barylko, Jaime. *La filosofía de Maimónides*, (Buenos Aires, 1985).

16. Orian, Meir. *Maimónides; vida, pensamiento y obra*, (Barcelona, 1984). Translated from Hebrew.

17. Crawford, James, "The Vision Delectable and Maimonides' 'Guide of the Perplexed'," Modern Language Association *Publications* 28 (1913): 188-212. On the influence of Maimonides on Alfonso de la Torre (1417-1460); cf. also T. and J. Carreras y Artau, *Historia de la filosofía española* (Madrid, 1943) II, 582-92; F. Secret, "Les Débuts du Kabbalisme chrétien en Espagne," *Sefarad* 17 (1947): 39ff.; Américo Castro, "Un aspecto del pensar hispano-judío," *Hispania* 35 (1052): 317-24.

In addition to the above works dealing specifically with Maimonides, information may be found in any of the standard Spanish encyclopedias, in all the works dealing with medieval Spanish philosophy, and some of those on literature (including older works, such as Menéndez Pelayo). As a result of this year's 850th Anniversary celebrations, we may expect new commemorative volumes of the Spanish conferences.

Maimonides as Spaniard: National Consciousness of a Medieval Jew

(I Congreso Internacional sobre la vida y obra de Maimónides, Córdoba, September 8-11, 1985)

In the times when religion played perhaps a more central role in the concerns of people than it does today, they tended to identify themselves more in terms of affiliation with their religious community than with any particular land. Even the nationalism of the Greeks and Romans was more cultural than patriotic. The world was divided into Greeks (later Romans) and barbarians, but the aspiration to Greek or Roman citizenship was not limited to residents of the country. It was available to those within the empire who could adapt themselves to Hellenistic, or Roman, culture and meet certain legal and political tests.[1]

For the early Jews, as well, although the Land of Israel remained always the national and spiritual homeland, the fact that the vast majority of Jews lived scattered throughout an ever expanding diaspora from the time of the first Babylonian conquest meant that they considered themselves part of a people, rather than citizens of a nation-state, the unifying element of which was religion and culture. This was to become increasingly important in the medieval period, and continues to be so today, as Jews spread even further throughout the lands of the world and not even a common language could any longer serve as a bond of the dispersed people. The Jews developed the notion, at a very early time (already in the Talmud) of *klal Yisrael* or *keneset Yisrael* ("community of Israel," or "assembly of Israel").[2] Similarly, and perhaps even influenced to some extent by the Jewish concept, the Christian notion of *Res publica christiana* saw the whole world as a Christian unity.[3]

There simply was no room for a modern idea of "tolerance"

in this medieval worldview, in fact; only at best a kind of uneasy coexistence with Jews and Muslims. With the latter, of course, this was only a temporary truce until the Christian Reconquest of Spain could begin in earnest, and the "infidels" now became "enemies of the faith" (*enemigos de la fe*) in earnest, and this term was soon applied to the Jews as well (although there was never any organized or government sanctioned warfare against the Jews in Spain, of course, and the term is restricted to theological and some legal documents).[4]

The Muslims, too, developed a strong sense of religious community which transcended national borders and was akin to, and again probably influenced by, the Jewish notion. There were also two powerful forces operating within the Muslim world which played a decisive role in the developing nationalism. One was *ᶜArabiyya*, or the idealization of the superiority of Arabic language and culture, resulting even in the falsification of claims to "pure" Arabic descent among the mostly Berber, Persian, and Syrian Muslims of Spain, and the other was the reaction against this very process which began in Persia and soon spread also to Spain.[5] There is no doubt that this latter process had much to do with the growing sense of real nationalism and patiotism of the Muslims of al-Andalus; combined, of course, with the independence of the Andalusian caliphate from that of Baghdad.

Already Aḥmad al-Rāzī praised the greatness of Spain; its numerous rivers and the quality of its water, its temperate climate, its mountains and forests—in short, it resembles Paradise. It has both sea and fresh water fish, all kinds of fruit and grains, etc.[6]

This kind of glorification of Spain was repeated frequently in the works of Spanish Muslims. For example, the twelfth-century historian al-Marrākushī notes that Spain is the capital of the West (*al-maghrib al-aqṣa*) and the source of its merits; the majority of talented people come from Spain, where science had its beginning. No region "has a more equal temperature, an air more pure, better water, more pleasantly aromatic plants, more abundant roses, more agreeable afternoons or sweeter evenings."[7] In the fourteenth-century, Ibn Hudhayl continued the same theme, noting that al-Andalus has the most pure sun and is made successful "by the accumulated merit of martyrdom" of its Muslim inhabitants, and concluded that "its history is extraordinary, and prevails over that of all other countries." (He then goes on, of course, to attack the Christian enemy, which was the chief purpose of his book.)[8] Even as late an author as al-Maqqarī (d. 1631), himself not a Spaniard, cited an Andalusian writer who called his land the Iraq of the West, in the beauty of its literature, excellence of its sciences, its poetry, and the general blessings of Allāh on the land: its rivers, mountains, wine, etc. Even al-Maqqarī added his own praise of the land he never saw.[9]

The Jews who lived in Spain far longer than they have lived in any other country in their history in the diaspora (indeed, almost as long as the ancient Israelites inhabited their land from the exodus and conquest to the Roman destruction of the Temple) were also not lacking in nationalist sentiment and praise of their native land. This theme of Jewish Spanish nationalism has never been adequately considered, just as the broader theme of medieval Spanish nationalism in general has yet to be fully detailed. The love of Spain's Jews for their country, the only country which provided them with security and equal protection under the law, or the closest thing that passed for it in the pre-modern world (which means that they truly enjoyed equality in most areas of life; let there be no mistake about that), has perhaps not been a popular subject for exploration at the hands of Jewish historians, many of whom have had their own nationalist biases and metaphysical visions of history to advance. It may not be too much to suggest, for instance, that this patriotism was a significant factor in the choice of the overwhelming majority of Jews who decided to convert to Christianity rather than face exile from their homes in 1492. Much has been written, often incorrectly, about the massive conversion of Jews throughout the fifteenth-century, but little effort has been made to distinguish between those who converted for various reasons prior to the order of expulsion and those who converted at the last minute rather than leave Spain.

One might have expected, too, that the exiles from Spain, who endured almost unimaginable hardships in trying to settle in new and strange lands, often in Arabic-speaking countries where they didn't even know the language, would have held a deep and bitter resentment of Spain which they would have passed on to their descendants. Such was not the case at all. We know that Spanish travelers in the fifteenth and sixteenth centuries expressed their astonishment at finding Jews in the Muslim world who spoke perfect medieval Castilian and proudly referred to themselves as "Spaniards." But this national pride persisted among the descendants of Spanish Jews well into recent times. The renowned literary scholar Guillermo Díaz-Plaja records that on his first visit to Salonica in 1933, the local rabbi to whom he was speaking called out (in Spanish) to a Jewish boy who was passing: "Little boy, where are you from?" His reply was, "I am a Catalan." The rabbi explained that actually the boy's family did originate in Tortosa, and they have remembered this for some five centuries.[10]

The Jews of Spain, who settled there at least in the third century C.E. and possibly earlier, had traditions according to which they had come much earlier—in the exile of Nebuchadnezzar, according to some, or even in the time of Solomon. They applied to their native land the biblical term *Sefarad* (Obadiah 20; where the Aramaic *Targum* translation of "Ispamia" may have been the source for this identification.)[11] Apparently the first source we have for this application of *Sefarad* to Spain is the famous letter of Ḥasdai Ibn Shapruṭ to the king of the Khazars, which opens with the words: "From me, Ḥasdai ben Yiṣḥaq ben ᶜEzra of the children of the exile of Jerusalem which is in *Sefarad*." At any rate, the identification quickly spread and became the standard term. It is interesting to note that, as far as I can determine, the Jews never used the name al-Andalus or the adjective *Andalūsī* in any of their Hebrew writings (both are found, of course, in Judeo-Arabic writings).[12] The term exclusively used was Sefarad, which Ibn Daud of

Toledo, for instance, repeatedly employed in his chronicle, and this refers *only* to Muslim Spain, and "land of the West" or simply "Edom" for Christian Spain.[13]

Unfortunately, we have less likelihood of finding significant references in the Hebrew writing of medieval Spain which would give evidence of a Jewish glorification of Spain similar to that among the Muslims. The reason is that Jews did not write geographies and descriptions of lands as the Muslims did. Even historical writing was extremely rare, and what little there was is mostly simple chronicles with not much embellishment. While Sefarad and Ispamia (Spain) figure frequently in the poetry of Ibn Naghrillah, but almost never in other Hebrew poetry, none of the citations is praising the country as such.

What is of interest for the present purpose is to consider the case of another exile from Spain, centuries before the period of the Inquisition and the massive conversion and exile of Jews. He, too, suffered a persecution of a different kind and from a different source: the Almohads. As a result of the Almohad invasion and the increasingly intolerable conditions for observant Jews in al-Andalus, Maimonides and his family (his father, a brother David, and a sister Miriam; presumably, his mother had died) left Spain and went first to Fez. Earlier scholars were fond of suggesting that this was a peculiar and dangerous move, for the Almohads already had control of Fez. We know, thanks to recent research, that in fact the situation for both Jews and Christians was much better in Fez than it was then in much of al-Andalus. Nor did this move have anything to do, of course, with the legendary conversion of Maimonides to Islam, long ago disproved but still subject to acceptance by some naive historians.[14]

The situation may have worsened in Fez, and at any rate, Maimonides went for a short period to Palestine, and finally settled in Fustat in Egypt. To his already growing fame as a legal scholar (his treatise on logic was written while still in Spain, and his commentary on the Mishnah was at least begun there), he now added fame as one of the greatest physicians of his time, winning the respect of Jews, Muslims and Christians, and began the composition of his great work, the **Mishneh Torah**. Questions on Jewish law soon poured in to him from many lands, including distant Provence. Maimonides was never a rabbi, yet he was the greatest Jewish legal authority. Scholars, of course, have investigated in considerable detail his commentary on the Mishnah, his **Mishneh Torah**, and to a lesser degree his legal responsa. Yet one question appears never to have been asked, and that is: How are we to explain the fact that, although he never returned to Spain, and although he had fled the country under the most adverse circumstances, he repeatedly refers to himself as "the Spaniard?" More than a mere signatory formula, he frequently alludes to "deeds which come before us" in Spain, when it fact he was sitting in Fustat.

First, let us assemble the evidence. In the opening of his introduction to his commentary on the Mishnah (which introduction was written, of course, after he had concluded the entire commentary, and thus long after he had left Spain), he says, "I am Moses b. Maimon *ha-Sefardy* [the Spaniard]."[15] In his responsum in reply to Obadyah the proselyte, he writes, "Moses b. Maimon of the children of the exile of Jerusalem in Sefarad," exactly as Ibn Shapruṭ had done in his letter to the king of the Khazars.[16]

Elsewhere in his responsa, he refers to "actual cases of law before us in all the communities [*bilād*; so, not "lands"] of al-Andalus always."[17] Now, it is highly unlikely that Maimonides had ever judged any cases of law when he was a teenager in al-Andalus; especially since his father was a noted *dayyan* (religious judge) of Córdoba in his own right. Rather we see that Maimonides still thought of himself as a Spaniard long after he had left Spain, and referred to events which happened in Spain as though he himself were still there. (In other responsa, he refers frequently to the customs and practices of the Jews in Spain, implying that these are a legal precedent for other communities.)

In the very important long letter of Maimondes to Pinḥas b. Meshullam of Alexandria, in the section concerning the Muslim practice of ablution for emissions before prayer, Maimonides says: "It happens constantly that scholars and rabbis of your city [Alexandria] *come* to Spain, and when they see *us* [i.e., inhabitants of Spain] washing because of seminal emissions they laugh at *us* and say, 'You learned from the cleansing of the Muslims'..."[18]

The most striking statement of all, however, is in his letter to Yafet (so, not "Yefet") b. Eliyahu, who had been a friend of Maimonides' family in Spain, in which he says: "You complain against me that I did not initiate enquiries as to your welfare from the day when we parted from the glorious land."[19] Now, the phrase "glorious land" usually refers to Palestine (Daniel 11.16, 41; but cf. Isaiah 13.19, where it is used of Babylon). Here, however, Maimonides clearly uses the expression to refer to *Spain* (as the context, which refers to the death of his father, which happened after Maimonides came to Egypt, indicates).

Maimonides did not always approve of the customs of the Jews of al-Andalus, and once speaks rather sharply against the religious poems (*azharot*) enumerating the commandments of the Torah "which were composed among us in Spain."[20] Generally, however, he was quite proud of his Spanish background. In fact, there is evidence to support the conclusion that he considered the Jews of al-Andalus in every way superior. For instance, in the *Guide of the Perplexed*, having given a rather confused and inaccurate account of he Muslim *kalām* (theological reasoning) of Islam, he boasts that "As for the Andalusians among the people of our nation [i.e., the Jews of Spain], all of them cling to the affirmations of the philosophers and incline to their opinions...You will not find them in any way taking the paths of the Mutakallimūn."[21] This is, of course, simply untrue and the gross exaggeration in this statement can only be explained as polemic not only against Islam, but against Jews elsewhere, who by implication are not smart enough to follow the Aristotelian philosophers and so do "take the paths" of the *kalām*.[22]

For the sake of completeness, we shall refer to one final statement by Maimonides, even though the text is extremely problematic in that, like several other letters, it is at least partly a forgery. This is the letter to his son, Abraham. I have studied this letter carefully, and the charges of forgery made against it, and I am not totally convinced that it is not authentic. It any case, it is interesting enough to mention here. At the close of the letter he warns his son: "Guard your soul very much from the words of the majority of the compositions of the men of France [he uses the Hebrew term *Ṣarfat*, followed by the vernacular *Franzah*, in order to make clear that he does not mean Provence], in which it does not appear that they recognize the Creator, may he be blessed, except at the time when they eat the boiled flesh of cattle dipped in vinegar and garlic, which is the dip called in their language *salsâ* [in Languedoc, a term for sauce, from which later came the same word in Spanish] and the vapor of the vinegar and the 'smoke' [fragrance] of the garlic ascend into their brains, and they think then to apprehend by this the Creator at every hour, and that he is close to them in their prayers and shouting in reading in the Talmud..." He continues: "And you, my son, do not let your pleasant association be other than with our brethren who love us, the Spaniards called Andalusians, for they have intelligence and understanding and the merit of a brain; others than they, be careful of them!" Strong as this criticism sounds to our ears, it is not at all improbable that Maimonides actually said this, for he elsewhere criticizes the scholars of France.[23]

On the other hand, Maimonides' reputation was not insignificant with French scholars. Since it has often erroneously been stated that Moses of Coucy (13th-century) was the first French rabbi to mention Maimonides, it needs to be re-emphasized here that this was not the case. Already in 1203 or 1204, Meir Abulafia addressed his letter attacking Maimonides to rabbis of France, and the renowned Samson of Sens (probably a teacher of Moses of Coucy) replied rebuking the young upstart Castilian and indicating that, even though there may be room to disagree with some of Maimonides' interpretations, generally he is to be followed. Thus, certainly, Samson had read and knew well the **Mishneh Torah**. Judah b. Isaac "Sire Léon" of Paris (ca. 1198), also a teacher of Moses of Coucy, already cited Maimonides. The French *Tosafot* (anonymously, but possibly also prior to Moses of Coucy) cite Maimonides at least twice.

Eliezer of Mitz, a student of Rabbenu Tam, also cited him. In Germany in the thirteenth-century he is cited by Rabbi Ele^{c}azar, *Sefer Roqeaḥ*, and in 1313 by Judah b. Eliezer, *Minhat Yehudah*. Thus, it is at least somewhat of an exaggeration to say that Maimonides' **Mishneh Torah** (and "its author") "certainly never became the cultural symbol [among the Ashkenazim] that he [it] was in" Spain.[24]

Maimonides, of course, left a profound influence in Spain. His works were widely known there even in his own lifetime, and the **Mishneh Torah** became the standard for Jewish practice (it is true that it never quite reached this level of importance in France). We find citations of his work on virtually every page of the novellae on the Talmud and in the responsa literature of Spanish Jewish rabbis throughout the medieval period, and this is none the less true for those, like Naḥmanides, who occasionally disagreed with him.

What is less well known, perhaps, is the impact which Maimonides had on the non-Jewish circles of Spain. Very little attention has been paid to the possible influence of Maimonides in Spanish Christian writing. Pedro of Toledo is known to have made a Spanish translation of the **Guide** for the first time, and this was the *first philosophic work* written in the Spanish language. The influence of Maimonides on Alfonso de Torre (1417-1460) has also been analyzed. It is of interest to note that among the manuscripts owned by Sancho, son of Jaime I of Aragon, archbishop of Toledo (1266-1275), we find "*Libro rabi Moyses cuius principium est Dixit Moyses egipcius*" (i.e., the **Guide** in Latin translation). Archbishop Gonzalo García Gudiel (1280-1299) also had a copy in his library.[25] The great irony of history, for the man who all his life took pride in being a "Spaniard," was that medieval Christians referred to him as "Moyses Aegyptius"—Moses of Egypt—a title which he never himself used.[26]

It undoubtedly would astonish Maimonides, but perhaps also delight him, that his native Spain has seen fit to so honor him: with the numerous anniversary volumes in Spanish in 1935, with the lovely statue in Córdoba (and the preservation of his house), with the translation of his work in Spanish (the most recent the splendid translation of the **Guide** by Prof. Gonzalo Maeso), and with this conference. He would probably be even more impressed with the vast and excellent nature of Spanish scholarship on Jewish studies which this "glorious land" has produced.

Notes

[1] The subject of nationalism in medieval Spain, and particularly as reflected in the writings of Spanish Jews, is a topic with which I hope to deal elsewhere at length.

[2] Surprisingly, the notion is not as extensive in the Talmud as might be supposed, and aside from the well-known comparison of *keneset Yisrael* to a dove (*Berakhot* 53b, *Sanhedrin* 95a, *Shabbat* 49a, *Giṭṭin* 45a), the few talmudic statements all come from Palestinian sages (*ᶜEruvin* 21b, *Pesaḥim* 87a, 118, *Megillah* 12b, *Sanhedrin* 102b, *ᶜA.Z.* 35a, *Ketuvot* 111b, *Taᶜanit* 4a). The term appears more frequently in medieval literature (particularly in the midrash Song of Songs Rabbah, and the Zohar); cf. also *Mekhilta*, "*Shirta*" (ed. and tr. [English] Jacob Lauterbach [Philadelphia, 1949] II, 29, line 97 and *ibid.*, p. 107, line 3).

[3] There is considerable literature on this subject, of course. See especially Gerhard Ladner, "The Concepts of 'Ecclesia' and 'Christianitas' and their relation to the idea of papal 'Plenitudo potestatis' from Gregory VII to Boniface VIII," *Sacerdozio e regno da Gregorio VII a Boniface VIII* (Miscellanea hist. pontificae XVIII, Rome, 1954), pp. 49-77; R. Manselli, "La 'Christianitas' medioevale di fronte all'eresia," *Studi sulle eresie del secolo XII* (Rome, 1975), pp. 293-327; his "La res publica Christiana et l'Islam," *L'Occident e l'Islam nell'alto medioevo* (Spolento, 1965) I, 115-47; F. Kempf, "Das Problem der Christianitas in 12-13 Jahrhunderts," *Historisches Jahrbuch* 79 (1960): 104-23; P. Rousset, "La Nation de Chrétienté aux XIe et XIIe siecles," *Moyen âge* 69 (1963): 191-203; and for a later period, but with important insights on the general subject, Franklin Baumer, "England, the Turk and the Common Corps of Christendom," *American Historical Review* 50 (1944): 26-48.

[4] Actually, the term *enemigos de la fe* applied to Jews was infrequent in medieval sources. It appears only once in canon law, *Decretals* C. 23. X. II, 20 (the letter of Alexander III to the king of Spain), and rarely in Spanish sources (e.g., *Cantigas de Santa Maria*, No. 348, line 48).

[5] See Roth, "Jewish Reactions to *ᶜArabiyya* and the

Renaissance of Hebrew in Spain," *Journal of Semitic Studies* 28 (1983 [1984]): 63-84, where the pertinent literature also for the Muslim aspect is cited.

[6] Aḥmad ibn Muḥammad ibn Mūsā al-Rāzī, *Crónica del Moro Rasis*, ed. Diego Catalán, et al. (Madrid, 1975), pp. 11-12; E. Lévi-Provençal, "La 'description de l'Espagne' d'Aḥmad al-Rāzī," *Al-Andalus* 18 (1953): 61-63.

[7] ᶜAbd al-Wāḥid al-Marrākushī, *Kitāb al-muᶜjib fī talkhīṣ akhbār al-maghrib*, ed. Reinhart P.A. Dozy (Leiden, 1881; photo rpt. Amsterdam, 1968), p. 115; *Histoire des Almohades*, tr. E. Fagnan (Alger, 1893), p. 138; tr. A. Huici Miranda (Tetuán, Colección de crónicas árabes de la reconquista IV, 1955), p. 119.

[8] ᶜAlī b. ᶜAbd al-Raḥmān Ibn Hudhayl, *L'ornement des âmes et la divise des habitants d'el Andalus*, tr. Louis Mercier (Paris, 1939), p. 119.

[9] Cited by Judah Barzilay, "*ᶜIyyunim be-divrey shiratenu ha-Sefardit*", in M.Z. Kaddari, et al., ed., *Sefer Barukh Kurzweil* (Tel-Aviv, 1975), pp. 309-10. This selection, strangely, does not appear in Pascual de Gayangos' translation of Aḥmad ibn Muḥammad al-Maqqarī, *The History of the Mohammedan Dynasties in Spain* (London, 1840-1843; photo rpt., N.Y., 1964), but see al-Maqqarī's own praise of Al-Andalus there, I. 87-88.

[10] Díaz-Plaja, *Rembrandt y la sinagoga española* (Barcelona, 1982), p. 110, n. 14.

[11] I am working on a book on relations between Jews, Muslims and Christians in medieval Spain, in which I will deal extensively with the legends of Jewish origins in Spain.

[12] The text of Ibn Shapruṭ's letter is widely reprinted; some editions which are easier to obtain than the very early ones include Simḥah Assaf, *Meqorot ve-meḥqarim be-toldot Yisrael* (Jerusalem, 1946), pp. 91-99; Judah ha-Levy, *Kuzari* (Buenos Aires, 1943), p. 197. The heading of one of the poems in Samuel Ibn Naghrillah's *Divan* (ed. Dov Jarden, [Jerusalem, 1966], p. 109, No. 33) does have "al-Andalus," but the original Arabic is lost and this is a later Hebrew translation. The only exception I have so far noted is one responsum of Joseph Ibn Megash

Teshuvot [Warsaw, 1870], No. 75, but this is also a Hebrew translation from the Arabic original.

[13] Abraham Ibn Daud, *Sefer ha-qabbalah, The Book of Traditions*, ed. and tr. Gerson Cohen (Philadelpha, 1967), Hebrew text, pp. 46, 49, 51, 58, 60, 62, 63, 70. It is incorrect to translate this simply "Spain" as Cohen did, for it refers only to Muslim Spain, and should therefore be translated "al-Andalus." For instance, one passage as translated has Ibn Abitur going "from Spain to Pechina" (p. 67 of the translation). Since Pechina, at the time an important port north of Almería, is certainly in "Spain," this makes no sense. The correct translation is "al-Andalus," since Pechina was part of a separate kingdom of Almería, and Ibn Daud apparently sought to distinguish it—not entirely correctly—from the rest of al-Andalus. Other problems of this sort will be explained more fully in my book.

[14] The true nature of the situation in Fez was demonstrated by David Corcos (Abulafia), "*Le-ofey yaḥasam shel sheiliṭey ha-Almuḥadun le-yehudim,*" *Zion* 32 (1967): 137-60, with English summary. The old legend of Maimonides' supposed conversion is repeated once again by Bernard Lewis, *The Jews of Islam* (Princeton, 1984), p. 100. His representation of Maimonides' position with regard to Christian and Muslim creeds there (p. 84) is equally a distortion.

[15] Moses b. Maimon, **Mishnah ᶜim peirush**..., ed. Joseph Kafiḥ (Jerusalem, 1963) I, fol 1 (Hebrew page number); **Haqdamot le-ferush ha-mishnah**, ed. M.D. Rabinowitz (Jerusalem, 1961), fol. 8 (Rabinowitz cites Azulay, *Shem ha-gedolim* [I. 70, 76] that Maimonides thus referred to himself to avoid confusion with another Moses b. *Jacob*; cf. on him Moses b. Maimon, **Teshuvot** [see next note] ed. Friemann, p. 8 and n. 12, and ed. Blau, II. 542 and n. 12).

[16] **Teshuvot ha-Rambam**, ed. Abraham Friemann (Jerusalem, 1934), p. 40, No. 42; ed. Judah Blau (Jerusalem, 1960) II, 548, No. 293.

[17] *Ibid.*, ed. Friemann, p. 166 (line 23); ed. Blau, II, 387.

[18] The letter appears only in **Qoveṣ teshuvot ha-Rambam**

ve-iggrotav, ed. Abraham Lichtenberg (Leipzig, 1859; photo rpt. Farnborough, England, 1969) f. 25b.

[19] *Ibid.*, Pt. II, 37d.

[20] Introduction to **Sefer ha-miṣvot** ("Book of the Commandments"), ed. Joseph Kafiḥ (Jerusalem, 1958), p. 4; ed. Charles Chavel (Jerusalem, 1981), p. 22. I have already shown in the chapter on Maimonides on language, that this complaint is not a general condemnation of poetry, as misunderstood by Twersky.

[21] **Guide** I. 71, tr. Shlomo Pines (Chicago, 1963), p. 177. See on this, with some caution, Harry Wolfson, "The Jewish Kalam," *The Seventy-Fifth Anniversary Volume of the Jewish Quarterly Review* (Philadelphia, 1967), p. 544 ff.

[22] Cf. the similar statement about "those who belong to our community" *ibid.*, p. 179. In an excellent article, Carlos Ramos has suggested that the reference here might specifically be to Baḥya Ibn Paquda ("Algunos aspectos de la personalidad y de la obra del judío Zaragozano Bahya ben Yosef Ibn Paquda," *Archivo de filología aragonesa* 3 [1950]: 154). Less enlightening are Wolfson's statements, evidently referring to the same passage, p. 547 of the article cited (among other things, it is not correct that on the issue of attributes there was "no difference" between the Muᶜtazilah and the philosophers; the former rejected the doctrine of attributes altogether).

[23] Letter in **Qoveṣ teshuvot**, pt. II, 40a-b. Criticism of its authenticity: Rapoport in *Ginzey nistarot* (Hebrew section of *Jeschurun*) 3, 51-54, and S. Sachs, *ha-Yonah* (recently reprinted), p. 88, and elsewhere. Salo Baron, "The Historical Outlook of Maimonides," rpt. in his *History and Jewish Historians* (Philadelphia, 1964), pp. 392-93, n. 169, too readily accepted that the entire letter is a forgery, nor did he distinguish there between the scholars of *Provence* (Lunel) and *France*. As against the scholars who have thought the letter a forgery, it should be noted that Leopold Zunz, *Zur Geschichte und Literatur* (Berlin, 1845; photo rpt. Hildesheim; N.Y., 1976), p. 199, accepted it as authentic. For another statement of Maimonides critical of French scholars, surely not forged, see

Qoveṣ teshuvot I, 26c (the previously cited letter to Pinḥas b. Meshullam). Note also Maimonides' commentary on *Giṭṭin* 5.8 (in th edition of Kafiḥ, and cf. the text as cited by Joseph Karo, "*Bet Yosef,*" on *Ṭur, Oraḥ ḥayyim* 135).

[24] The error concerning Moses of Coucy may be based on a misunderstanding originating in H.J. Zimmels, *Ashkenazim and Sephardim* (London, 1956), p. 19. See Israel Ta-Shem in *Qoveṣ al-yad* 18 (n.s. 8) (1975): 167 for the specific statement that Moses of Coucy was the first to cite Maimonides. Abulafia's exchange with Samson of Sens and others is very casually (and unsatisfactorily) treated by Daniel Silver, *Maimonidean Criticism and the Maimonidean Controversy* (Leiden, 1965), p. 123, and no less so by Bernard Septimus, *Hispano-Jewish Culture in Transition* (Cambridge, Mass., 1982), pp. 48-49. It is unfortunate that neither author saw Ephraim Urbach, *Baᶜaley Tosafot* (Jerusalem, 1968; 3rd ed.), p. 226 and p. 259 (n. 117) which presents a more correct picture. Urbach suggests, correctly, that Judah b. Isaac "Sire Léon" was in fact the first French rabbi to cite Maimonides (*ibid.*, p. 272). The *Tosafot, Berakhot* 44a (*ᶜAl ha-ᶜeṣ*") *Menaḥot* 42b ("*Tefillin*"), unmentioned in Urbach, also cite Maimonides. For Eliezer of Mitz and Eleᶜazar, the *Roqeaḥ*, see Urbach pp. 139 and 325-26. Judah b. Eliezer, *Minḥot Yehudah* (Livorno, 1783), f.51a and 82b. The claim that Maimonides was less a "cultural symbol" in France than Spain is by Septimus, *op. cit.*, p. 49.

[25] Bibliography of Pedro of Toledo's translation (an edition now being prepared by Prof. Moshé Lazar) and on Alfonso de Torre can be found in the chapter "Maimonides and Spanish Scholarship" On the Spanish-owned manuscripts of the **Guide** mentioned, see J.M. Millás Vallicrosa, *Las traducciones orientales en los manuscritos de la Biblioteca Catedral de Toledo* (Madrid, 1942), pp. 16 and 17.

[26] See the very important study of Wolfgang Kluxen, "Literargeschichtliches zum lateinischen Moses Maimonides," *Recherches de théologie ancienne et médiévale* 21 (1954): 23-50.

Maimonides: Basic Bibliography and a Proposal

In addition to the bibliographies in English and in Spanish, it seemed that it might be helpful to include also a general bibliography of the basic works of Maimonides, excluding his medical writings (reference to most of these can be found in the works cited on Maimonides as physician in the chapter on his impact on world culture). This is by no means an attempt at a complete bibliography of all the editions and translations of Maimonides' work, which has never yet been done (such a listing will appear in the catalogue of all published works by Jewish authors of medieval Spain on which I have been working for many years). Rather, it lists only major editions: critical editions, editions with important commentaries, etc., and English translations which are more or less easily accessible.

I. Commentary on the Mishnah (*Kitāb al-sarāj; Sefer ha-me'or*)

1. Judeo-Arabic Texts

   a. First complete edition, with Latin translation, *Mischna, sive totius Hebraeos juris*, ed. and tr. G. Surenhusius (Amsterdam, 1698-1703).
   b. Individual editions of separate tractates, usually also with the medieval Hebrew translation, appeared in Germany in the nineteenth century. They are of uneven quality. A listing of these may be found in *Moses Maimonides' Commentary on the Mishnah. Introduction to Seder Zeraim and Commentary on Berachoth*, tr. Fred Rosner (N.Y., 1975), pp. 25-30.
   c. Probable autograph ms. of Maimonides, *Maimonidis' Commentarius in Mischnam* ed. S.D. Sassoon (Murksgaard, 1956-61)
   d. *Partial* edition of Judeo-Arabic texts in *Mishnah ᶜim*

peirush rabbeinu Mosheh ben Maimon (see 2.d. below).

e. *Maimonides' Commentary on the Mishnah Tractate Sanhedrin*, tr. Fred Rosner (N.Y., 1981).

2. Hebrew Translations

a. Naples, 1492 (*editio princeps*, of Orders I and II only, of medieval Hebrew translations); photo rpt. Jerusalem, 1970, with intro. A.M. Habermann.

b. Riva di Trento, 1559 (Orders IV, V, VI, medieval Hebrew translations).

c. Most editions of *Talmud Bavli* with commentaries contain these Hebrew translations, but the text is not always reliable.

d. *Mishnah ᶜim peirush rabbeinu Mosheh ben Maimon*, ed. and tr. Joseph Kafiḥ (not "Kapaḥ") (Jerusalem, 1963-69). For some reason, the intent to include also the original Judeo-Arabic text was never completed. The Hebrew translation is original.

e. *Mishnah* (Ms. Parma, De Rossi 984) with commentary of Maimonides (facsimile ed., Jerusalem, 1971). *Nashim* and *Neziqin* only.

3. Introductions to Commentaries on the Mishnah

a. *Porta Mosis sive dissertationes...Moses Maimonides*, ed. (Arabic) and tr. (Latin) Edward Pococke (Oxford, 1655).

b. *Haqdamot le-feirush ha-mishnah* (Hebrew tr.), ed. M.D. Rabinowitz (Jerusalem, 1961, with numerous reprints).

c. *Moses Maimonides' Commentary on the Mishnah: Introduction to Seder Zeraim and Commentary on Tractate Berachoth*, tr. Fred Rosner (N.Y., 1975). The translation is from the medieval Hebrew, not the original Judeo-Arabic text.

d. Introduction to *Pirqey Avot* and/or Commentary:

1. Judeo-Arabic text, ed. E. Baneth in Lehranstalt für die Wissenschaft des Judenthums. *Dreiundzwanziger Bericht* (Berlin, 1905).
2. *Acht Kapitel*, ed. and tr. (German) Maurice Wolff (Leiden, 1903; photo rpt. Hamburg, 1981).
3. *The Eight Chapters of Maimonides on Ethics* (the Introduction), tr. Joseph I. Gorfinkle (N.Y., 1912).
4. *The Commentary to Mishnah Aboth*, tr. Arthur David (N.Y., 1968). Translation based on Hebrew translation only; very unreliable.

II. Code of Jewish Law (*Mishneh Torah*)

1. Editions (Hebrew original)

a. s.l.s.a. (Italy, before 1480); photo rpt. Jerusalem, 1955.
b. Soncino, 1490; photo rpt. Jerusalem, 1975.
c. Constantinople, 1509 (first edition with the standard medieval commentaries); photo rpt. Jerusalem 1972. (4 vols.)
d. Vilna, 1900 (major edition, with numerous additional commentaries); photo rpt. N.Y., 1947, with additions from autograph mss., responsa of Maimonides and his son Abraham, etc. There are various other reprints of the Vilna edition; e.g., N.Y., 1975; Jerusalem, 1972.
e. Jerusalem, 1964 (critical edition, ed. Jacob Cohen, M. Katzenellenbogen, *et al.*; never completed).
f. *A Majmoni Kodex* (Budapest, 1980); facsimile edition of Kaufmann Genizah mss.

2. English Translations

a. *The Book of Knowledge* and *The Book of Adoration*, ed. and tr. Moses Hyamson (London, 1940; rpts. 1949, 1962, etc.)
b. *Mishneh Torah* (New Haven, Yale Judaica Series, 1951—). Eventually will be a complete translation.
c. *The Book of Knowledge from the Mishnah* [sic] *Torah of Maimonides*, tr. H.M. Russell and J. Weinberg (Edinburgh, 1981). An improvement over Hyamson's translation, but still not accurate.

III. **Book of Commandments (*Sefer ha-mişvot*)**

1. Editions and Hebrew Translations

a. *Livre des préceptes*, ed. Moses Bloch (Paris, 1888).
b. *Sefer ha-mişvot*, ed. Hayyim Heller (Piotrkow, 1914; revised ed., Jerusalem, 1946). Hebrew translation of Moses Ibn Tibbon, ed. according to mss. with "corrections" according to Arabic text; also Hebrew tr. of Solomon Ibn Ayyūb. The Hebrew tr. of Ibn Tibbon only, ed. Heller (Jerusalem, 1980).
c. Hebrew tr., corrected according to Arabic text, ed. Joseph Kafiḥ (Jerusalem, 1958).
d. Judeo-Arabic text, ed. with new Hebrew translation by Joseph Kafiḥ (Jerusalem, 1971).
e. Hebrew translation, based on Constantinople, ca. 1510 edition, with strictures of Moses b. Naḥmanides), ed. Charles Chavel (Jerusalem, 1981).

2. English translations

a. *The Commandments*, tr. Charles Chavel (Jerusalem-N.Y., 1967).

IV. **Treatise on Logic (*Millot ha-higgayon*)**

a. *Bi'ur millot ha-higgayon* (Warsaw, 1865; rpt. Berlin, 1928). Text of Hebrew translation of Moses Ibn Tibbon, with important commentaries by Mordecai Contino and Moses Mendelssohn, ed. Isaac Satanov and David Slucki.
b. Edition of Judeo-Arabic text, medieval Hebrew translations, with English tr., Israel Efros (N.Y., 1938 [American Academy for Jewish Research. *Proceedings*. 8])
c. Hebrew translation of Ibn Tibbon, ed. Leon Roth (Jerusalem, 1965).
d. Original Arabic, based on new ms., "*Maqālah fī ṣinaᶜat al-manṭiq*," ed. Mubahat Türker (with Turkish tr.) in *Ankara Universitesi Dil ve Tarih-Coğrafaya Fakültesi Dergisi* 18 (1960): 40-64.
e. Text-re-ed. Israel Efros, based on d., in American Academy for Jewish Research. *Proceedings* 34 (1966): 155-60 and 17 pp. of text.

V. **Guide of the Perplexed (*Moreh Nevukhim*)**

1. Editions

a. *Le Guide des égarés*, ed. (Judeo-Arabic) and tr. Salomo Munk (Paris, 1856-66; photo rpt. Osnabrück, 1964; Paris, 1970).
b. Hebrew tr. of Judah al-Ḥarizi, ed. S. Munk *et al.*, (London, 1879; rpt. Tel-Aviv, 1964).
c. Hebrew translation (Vienna, 1828), with commentaries of Moses Narboni and Solomon Maimon.
d. Hebrew translation (Vilna, 1904 and frequent reprints), with the standard commentaries of Shem Tov b. Joseph Ibn Shem Tov, Asher b. Abraham

(Bonan Crescas), Isaac b. Moses ha-Levy (Profiat Duran), Isaac Abravanel.

e. Judeo-Arabic text (Jerusalem, 1931), Munk's text, revised by I. Joel.

f. New Hebrew translation, Yehudah Even-Shmuel (Tel-Aviv, 1935-38; rpt. Jerusalem, 1958-60). Parts I and II only were completed. Important notes.

2. English translations

a. *The Guide for the Perplexed*, tr. M. Friedlander (London, 1881-85; 3 vols.). Translated from Hebrew only. Often reprinted in 1-vol. edition lacking the important introductions and notes.

b. *The Guide of the Perplexed*, tr. Shlomo Pines (Chicago, 1963; 1969). Translated from Arabic.

c. Selections, in *Rambam, Readings in the Philosophy of Maimonides*, tr. Lenn E. Goodman (N.Y., 1976). New translations from the Arabic; hardly an improvement on Pines, but may be easier for the general reader to follow.

VI. *Letters, Theological Treatises*

1. Editions and Translations

a. *Qoveṣ teshuvot ha-Rambam ve-iggrotav* (not *"iggerotav"*) ed. Abraham Lichtenberg (Leipzig, 1859; photo rpt. Farnborough, England, 1969). Contains all letters and theological treatises, etc.

b. *Iggrot ha-Rambam*, ed. D.H. Baneth (Jerusalem, 1946). Texts of letters, ed. from mss. Contains only two of those found already in a. above: letter to Joseph Ibn Shimᶜon (f. 29 b-c of Lichtenberg; p. 24 of Baneth), and the complete text of the (suspicious, perhaps forged) letter to him (f. 30c-31d of

Lichtenberg; p. 49 ff. of Baneth). All the other letters are published by Baneth for the first time, or re-edited on the basis of new mss.

c. *Iggrot ha-Rambam*, ed. M.D. Rabinowitz (Jerusalem, 1968). Contains "Epistles on Apostasy," "Epistle to Yemen," "Treatise on Resurrection" (probably a forgery).

d. *Iggrot*, ed. and tr. Joseph Kafiḥ (Jerusalem, 1972). Only edition with original Arabic texts, and with Hebrew tr. based on them, by Kafiḥ. Contains "Epistle to Yemen," "Treatise on Resurrection," "Epistle to Joseph Ibn Shim^{c}on," "Introduction to Commentary on Aphorisms of Hippocrates," and ch. 1 of "Medical Aphorisms" (contrary to Kafiḥ there, these have been previously published).

e. *Rabbeninu Mosheh ben Maimon, iygrrotav* [sic] *ve-toldot ḥayyav*, ed. Mordechai Bar-Joseph (Tel-Aviv, 1970; privately published). This peculiarity is mentioned only because it has been made available to college libraries. It is an anthology of letters and theological treatises, "edited" by Mr. Bar-Joseph (i.e., abridged and re-written in "modern" Hebrew). It is absolutely without scholarly value.

f. *Iggeret le-Teiman. Epistle to Yemen*, ed. and tr. A.S. Halkin and B. Cohen (N.Y., 1952). Judeo-Arabic text, with medieval Hebrew translations, and English translation (unfortuntely from the Hebrew only, and thus not always reliable).

g. *Ma'amar teḥiyyat ha-metim. Maimonides' Treatise on Resurrection*, ed. (Judeo-Arabic and Hebrew translation of Samuel Ibn Tibbon) Joshua Finkel (N.Y., 1939). Strangely, no English translation of this important, but probably spurious, work. See now h. below.

h. *Treatise on Resurrection*, tr. Fred Rosner (N.Y., 1982). Translation from the Hebrew only.

i. "Letter on Astrology," Hebrew text ed. A. Marx in *Hebrew Union College Annual* 3 (1926): 311-58, and cf. 4 (1927): 493-94. English translation by Ralph Lerner in Lerner and Muhsin Mahdi, eds., *Medieval Political Philosophy* (Glencoe, Ill., 1963; Ithaca, N.Y., 1963, 1972), pp. 227-36.

j. *Letters of Maimonides*, tr. (from Hebrew only) Leon Stitskin (N.Y. 1977).

VII. *Responsa*

a. *Qoveṣ teshuvot ha-Rambam* (see VI.a.).

b. *Teshuvot ha-Rambam*, ed. A. Freimann (Jerusalem, 1934). Scholars tend now to ignore this edition, but it contains very valuable notes.

c. *Teshuvot ha-Rambam*, ed. and tr. Joshua Blau (Jerusalem, 1958). Judeo-Arabic text with Hebrew translations.

d. *Maimonides on Listening to Music*, ed. and tr. H. Farmer (Bearsden, Scotland, 1941). Texts of responsa, commented upon by authority on medieval music.

VIII. *Astronomical Works*

a. *Ma'amar ha-ᶜibbur. Die ältesten astronomische Schrift des Maimonides*, tr. L. Dünner (Würzburg, 1902).

b. Hebrew text in *Qoveṣ teshuvot* (see VI.a.). (In addition, it is important to consult the relative treatises of the Code of Jewish Law, and also scattered references in the *Guide*, etc.)

Two "Modest Proposals"

It is obvious that, 850 years after the birth of Maimonides, we are still in a bad way with regard to critical editions, and English translations based on such editions, of his work. Aside from the **Guide**, the **Book of Commandments**, the Treatise on Logic, some of the letters and responsa, only his medical works have finally succeeded to have critical editions and careful translations. Therefore, there is a desperate need for the following projects to be undertaken.

1. A complete critical edition of the Judeo-Arabic mss. of the Commentary on the Mishnah, including all of the introductions (and a re-edition of the Eight Chapters on *Pirqey Avot*). For whatever reason, Kafiḥ did not complete this as is necessary; however admirable his Hebrew translation may be, there is no substitute for the original text. Scholars must determine whether the Copenhagen ms. is an authentic holograph or not, and it must be compared with other extant and previously published mss.

2. Complete English translations of the Introductions to the Commentary on the Mishnah, based solely on the original Arabic texts.

3. A complete critical edition of the Code (**Mishneh Torah**) in the original Hebrew, with a critical edition of the most important medieval Hebrew commentaries (it is astonishing that, while the *Editio Princeps* has been photographically reproduced, as well as the first edition of some of the commentaries, there has still been no attempt to collate mss. either of the text itself or of the commentaries). However admirable (?) the English translations being undertaken in the Yale Judaica Series, a critical text of this all-important work seems even more crucial.

4. New editions (and in some cases, editions for the first time) are needed of all the commentaries on the **Guide**. Some of these are extremely rare and difficult to obtain, and many were issued in editions of dubious quality.

5. The Letters and Theological Treatises need thorough

investigation to determine which are authentic and which are forgeries (in part or in whole), and to establish authentic texts. All of these, including the "Epistle to Yemen" (which are translated solely from the Hebrew medieval versions), need to have careful English translations based on the original texts.

Secondly, as mentioned in the chapter in this book on Maimonides' Arabic Sources, the time has surely come for a serious cooperative effort by scholars of Greek and early Christian philosophy, of Muslim philosophy, and of Jewish philosophy to bring their efforts to bear on the complicated problem of the sources utilized by Maimonides in the **Guide** and in other of his philosophical writings (such as the introductions to the commentaries on the Mishnah). Years of annotating my own copies of the **Guide** and other works of Maimonides have shown me how difficult this task of locating definite and possible sources can be. We have waited in vain for years for someone to provide guidance in this direction, with no results. Neither the remarks in the very learned articles of Wolfson and others, nor the notes in Even-Shmuel's edition, are adequate. Pines failed to provide any but the most vague and general notes to his translation, and a long introduction, which is also of limited value. Munk's notes, however valuable, were limited necessarily by the knowledge available at his time. Few Muslim scholars have devoted attention to Maimonides, but the cogent insights of those who have (like Fakhry in his book on *Islamic Occasionalism*) are promising for what could be accomplished.

There surely could be no finer tribute to the memory of Maimonides in this 850th anniversary year than to begin preparations for both these projects.

The Hebrew & Semitic Studies Department of the University of Wisconsin, although it could not obviously undertake such a task alone, is willing to assist in the initiation of such a project. I look forward to hearing from those interested.

Index

Arabic terms discussed

Hebrew terms discussed

Ysopete-Zaragoza, 1489

hic liber confectus est
Madisoni .mcmlxxxv.